Reflections

Psalm 126
Living in heaven's light

Chris Hughes

DayOne

ENDORSEMENTS

Written in an engaging style – often humorous – this book takes us on a journey into a deeper understanding of this great Psalm. Setting it in its historical context – with detailed exposition, helpful illustration, and compelling application – Chris Hughes, as always, brings God's Word alive for the twenty-first-century Christian.

Jim Winter (Retired Pastor and Day One Council member)

The Psalms are often quite personal, and Chris uses some of his own personal reflections as he opens this particular Psalm to us. He provides the historical and cultural context which helps the reader understand the modern application. The questions in the 'Reflection' section also challenge us to think about the application in everyday life. I can commend this book as being useful for both personal and group study.

Don Olden (Pastor of Koinonia Evangelical Church, Andover)

Chris takes us on a personal journey over his forty years walking with Christ. This thoughtful journal faithfully expounds Psalm 126, drawing out wise and practical implications that are signposts for all of our lives.

Lyndon Bowring (Chairman of CARE – Christian Action Research & Education)

Chris Hughes combines deep theological insight with rich practical application in this absorbing study of the 'Pilgrim Song', Psalm 126. He shows vividly how Israel's experience of exile and hope of restoration is reflected in the Psalm, and how this informs Jesus' subsequent life and work of salvation. Along the way, he weaves in stories from his own and others' journeys of faith to demonstrate the enduring relevance of the Psalmist's words to present-day discipleship and mission. Each chapter ends with helpful questions for reflection that emphasize Chris' heart for godly action and lifestyle as well as for sound interpretation. Read this with the Psalm open in your Bible and you are sure to be blessed and strengthened in the conviction that 'The Lord has done great things for us'.

David Hilborn (Academic Dean—London School of Theology)

From just six verses of a Psalm, Chris is able to draw on the width of Scripture, personal experience and a broad context as a springboard to the whole Christian message, along with a personal challenge to the reader.

Stephen Spurgeon (Chair of Trustees Rural Ministries)

In this short and very readable book, Chris does an excellent job of helping his readers ascend the heights of Psalm 126. He takes great care to set it within its wider biblical context and to show us how it fits into the sweep of salvation history. But with great skill, he also allows this little portion of God's Word to teach, rebuke, correct and train us in righteousness, with the aid of some helpful personal insights and illustrations from his own life and ministry.

Jonathan Berry, (Minister and Team Leader—Above Bar Church, Southampton)

A delightful guide through one of my favourite Psalms by one of my dearest friends. Carefully handled, amply illustrated, and full of wise, practical, and personal application. Take and enjoy this journey through one of the Songs of Ascents!

Dr Steve Brady (Senior Pastor—First Baptist Church of Grand Cayman, West Indies)

Copyright © 2023 by Day One Publications

First published in Great Britain in 2023 by
Day One, Ryelands Road, Leominster, HR6 8NZ
Email: sales@dayone.co.uk
Website: www.dayone.co.uk

British Library Cataloguing in Publication Data available

ISBN: 978-1-84625-767-4

Cover design by Kathryn Chedgzoy

Printed by 4edge

CONTENTS

INTRODUCTION

Rudyard Kipling said, in connection with the story of the Elephant's Child:

> I keep six honest serving-men (They taught me all I knew); Their names are What and Why and When And How and Where and Who. I send them over land and sea, I send them east and west; But after they have worked for me, I give them all a rest.[1]

For our purposes in studying Psalm 126 and the Jewish travellers who would have sung it, we will need the help of three of these men:

- *Where* … where were they looking?
- *What* … what did they use?
- *How* … how were they to live?

In the first section of this book, we will look at the Where. After this, we will come back to the start of the Psalm and look at the What and then the How.

I have one request: No peeking!

We live in a world where 'How to' books can make the list of international best sellers. But there are two good reasons why simply jumping to the 'How' section is not recommended:

- You may be disappointed—I am not expecting this book to get onto anyone's best-seller list. Ultimately the 'How' is something that each one of us has to work out in the places where God calls us to follow Him. All we can do in this book is put up some signposts using what God says in this Psalm.

- More importantly, Jesus reminds us (in the story of the wise and foolish builders) that foundations are really important (Matt. 7: 24–27). Paul goes on to talk to early Christians in Corinth about how important it is to build on the one, true foundation (1 Cor. 3: 10–11).

So, in the first two sections of this book, we will dig down to examine some foundations and then work up from them and apply that examination in the third section.

Back~seat drivers

Every summer for about seven or eight years, my parents would pack the car for the start of a two-week holiday in a seaside town on the south coast of England. We stayed in the same place, hired a beach hut on the same strip of beach, went to watch the same Punch & Judy Show and walked, swam and played in the same places as we had done the previous year—and the year before that.

I am not sure that, as children, we recognized the same landmarks on the journey to our holiday destination but, at some point on the journey, either my brother or I would ask a rather plaintive question from the back seat of the car: 'Are we nearly there yet?'

I do not know whether it was the quality of the roads when I was a child, or the way cars were built in those days, or simply the time sense or attention span of a child, but journeys seemed to go on for ever.

Jumping forward a generation, my wife and I took a group of young people from our church on a short holiday in the countryside, along with some other adults. The roads were a bit better than in my childhood—as were the cars we used—but about halfway through the journey came the first cry of, 'Are we nearly there yet?'

As we came closer to our journey's end on the narrow and windy country roads, the cry from our young daughter changed to, 'Crash!' However, that was a comment on my driving and not what actually happened!

I ought to ask my son, who lives in America, whether

'Are we nearly there yet?' is something his children ask on long journeys.

A journey

Psalm 126 is about a journey. It is a journey that can be seen in a number of ways:

1. For the original Psalmist it was a real journey at a specific time in history with a clear picture of the geographical end to the journey.

We are not told in the Psalm itself exactly when the journey took place. C. H. Spurgeon in his book, *The Treasury of David*, puts it like this:

> There is nothing in this Psalm by which we can decide its date, further than this—that it is a song after a great deliverance from oppression.[1]

Nor are we helped by differences in translation between a focus on the captives ('who are brought back to Zion'—NIV) or the city ('the captivity of Zion'—AKJV) in verse 1.

However, there was only one period in Old Testament history when Jerusalem had both become the Jewish capital city, and had also been captured and its people taken away into captivity. It was the one and only time of God's promise of return or restoration being fulfilled. This was the series of captures and exiles starting in the reign of King Nebuchadnezzar of Babylon and the gradual restoration begun by King Cyrus of Persia.

It is against that background that these reflections can begin.

2. As the sub-heading of the Psalm indicates, this is one of the 'Songs of Ascents' ('Songs of Degrees' in the AKJV).

These songs start in Psalm 120 and carry on through to Psalm 134. Again, commentators and others give different answers as to why they were grouped together in the way that they are and also how they were used.[2]

In my opinion, the most likely answers as to how they were used appears to be:

- Levites chanting them as they mounted the steps to the Temple.

- Their wider use by those on pilgrim journey to Jerusalem to stand inside the Temple Courts (Psalm 134—the end of journey—is set in the house of the Lord, in the sanctuary). Of those who have sung these 'Songs of Ascents' over the centuries, relatively few would come from the Jewish tribe of Levi. Even among those of the Levitical tribe, only a portion have had the opportunity of walking up the steps of the Temple in Jerusalem. However, there are many, many people (me included) who are able to find in these Psalms, and specifically in Psalm 126, things that are profitable for teaching, rebuking, correcting and training in righteousness (2 Tim. 3:16).

This Psalm speaks about our journey with God towards the home He has prepared for us to enjoy with Him. It is this aspect of the Psalm which is going to form the heart of our reflections.

However, we could also see it in the wider canvas of God's whole salvation plan. This would start at the beginning of time as humanity was taken captive by sin and banished from the place where they could walk with God in the cool of the day (Gen. 3:8). It would end where, once again, God's rescued people will see His face (Rev. 22:4), His throne will be in the city—i.e., He will be among them (v. 3) and He will give them light (v. 5), for there will be no more night (v. 5).

But how long is the journey?

In the days when we used maps to plan a journey (rather than simply tapping a destination into a satnav device), it was always hard to tell exactly how long any journey would take.

More recently, when I was coming home from work, my wife would often ask, 'When does your satnav say you will get home?' Most of the time the estimate it gave was reasonably accurate—but I remember well a journey that, because of snow, took over four times as long as it should have done and I feared that I would be stranded somewhere between work and home. The best satnav in the world could not have allowed for that.

The journey in Psalm 126 could be seen as taking:

- A matter of months—this being the period that it took Ezra to reach Jerusalem from Susa (the capital City of the Persian Empire): the difference between Ezra 7:8 (which tells us when he arrived in Jerusalem) and Ezra 7:9 (when he started his journey).

- Some seventy years—the period of exile spoken about by the prophet Jeremiah (Dan. 9:2). There were some who remembered seeing the Temple that had been destroyed, when the foundations for the new Temple were laid at the end of that seventy-year period (Ezra 3:12).

- A lifetime—or at least the period between a person becoming a Christian and the end of his or her life here on earth.

- All of time—from the very beginning of human history to the day when the Lord Jesus Christ winds up the history of this world and this universe and ushers in a New Heaven and a New Earth. For, in that New Heaven and New Earth, some of the things pictured in this Psalm will no longer exist (among them barren desert land, tears and the hard work of sowing and reaping).

But how far along that journey are we?

Can we know if we are 'nearly there yet' if we do not actually know when the journey will come to an end?

What we can know is the start of the journey. Have we actually started on the journey?

One cause of sadness in the Book of Ezra is that not everyone who received the invitation to start on the journey actually did so.

The invitation is seen in Ezra 1:1–4 (this is also found in 2 Chronicles 36:22–23). It was a political decision made by Cyrus to help secure his position of power when the Persians replaced the Babylonians as the 'superpower' of their day. It was not restricted to the Jewish people and there is a physical example of that invitation to another people which can be found in the British Museum today (it is known as the Cyrus Cylinder[3]).

But the list of those who responded to the invitation was relatively small—we see it in Ezra 2 and especially v. 64: there were only 42,360 people out of a whole nation who had been carried off into exile.

Personal reflections

I would like to reflect on two things relating to what we have looked at and then invite you to reflect on some things yourself:

MAKING AN IMPACT

As I look back on my life, I remember a specific comment made in a history lesson at school. It was in the last year of my time at school (and so I was about eighteen years old). We were studying a period of history recorded by a man called Herodotus—who was sometimes called the 'Father of History'[4]. He wrote about events during a time of conflict between the Persian Empire and the Greek peoples and States (Sparta and Athens among them). These conflicts are remembered many times a year when one particular race is run. The legend is that the distance of this race is the distance between the site of a great Greek victory against the Persians and Athens—the distance run by a messenger called Pheidippides who carried news of the victory to his people at home. The victory was at a place called Marathon.[5]

One day in our history class, the teacher said something quite simple. It was along the lines of, 'Of course, you can read about these events in the Bible.' I had never thought of the Bible in those terms before, that it was a Book of History—a Book that truly and accurately recorded the events of days past in human history.

A phrase that used to be used when wanting to emphasize that something was really, truly, totally and accurately correct was that it was 'the gospel truth'. An online dictionary puts it this way:

It is 'something that is thought to be as true as the biblical *gospel* (that is, undeniably true)'.[6]

The teacher's comment started a chain of events that brought me to look again at that gospel truth—by reading one of the Gospels—and through that, and other means, brought me to know the truth of the gospel in my own heart and life.

Just a simple comment—but, for me, what an impact it had!

WHEN WILL THE JOURNEY END?

During my time serving a wonderful group of God's people near Southampton in Hampshire, I had the privilege of getting to know something of the lives of a number of those people. Some I only knew for a short time as they were coming to the end of their journey here on earth when we moved into the area. Others had much of their journey behind them before we arrived—and yet others were still at an early stage on that journey. Two of them spring to mind:

One man was opposed to the Christian message for much of his adult life. People spoke of the times that his wife was accompanied home after an evening meeting because they were concerned about what might happen to her if she went home alone. However, at the time when most people think about retirement, he went with his wife for a holiday—helping to run a Children's Mission, working alongside a Missioner who had worked in the Hampshire area for many years. The Mission was for children but this man in his sixties found that God spoke to him through that time of mission and he became one of the most devoted and passionate members of the church. When I came to know him—some thirty years later—he had proved to be a wonderful servant of his Saviour and the local church in many different ways over the decades since his journey with God began. At the very end of his life, when his body was restricted by age and ill health, there were two things that he loved. One was to have access to a packet of Mint Imperials. The other was to be able to pray or join in with the prayers of others. When a time of prayer came to an end, his face beamed with a grin that appeared to spread almost from ear to ear. He was truly someone who knew that God had done a great thing for him—and there was no disguising that he was truly glad.

The other man had been brought up in a local church and had what he described as a clear experience of God in his life when he was in his teenage years. Sadly, however, things had gone wrong and, while his wife and children were part of the church, he kept away from any formal part of the church's life. Not that this meant he was unaware of Christian things—the church's young people were welcomed in their home, the ministers of the church over many years visited him and spent time with him, and a copy of Holman Hunt's picture of Jesus as the 'Light of the World' had a prominent place in the house's front hall. But, and it was a very big but, his journey, if it had ever started, had stalled. One thing that marked this stagnation was a time spent talking about the crucifixion of Jesus and the simple request made by one of the others being crucified that day (Luke 23:42): 'Jesus, remember me.' Could he ask Jesus to remember him? No—that was just not possible for him. And that remained true for a number of the years that I knew him. Then he became ill and, on a day in his hospital ward, I thought that he said he had asked Jesus to remember him. Later that day, one of his daughters saw him and came away with the clear and undoubted certainty that he had indeed asked his Saviour to remember him—the next day he saw his Saviour face to face. What a short journey! But a journey that reached the same end—the end that the thief hanging next to Jesus had been promised: to be with Christ in paradise (Luke 23:43).

These two men are among a multitude without number of men and women, young and old, people from every tribe and people and language, who have found, both in the life we have on earth and also when they have stepped through death into eternity, that God has indeed done great things for us. And of all these things the greatest is God's wonderful work of salvation. A salvation that finds its completion in the home prepared for us by Christ in paradise and the New Heaven and New Earth which are yet to come.

People start that journey with God at different times in their lives, God uses different means to bring people to the start of that journey. I am amazed that God used the means that he did in my life, in the lives of members of my family, in the lives of those two men and in many other Christians from different places around the world that it has been my privilege to come to know.

For reflection

1. *Are you on that journey with God?*

2. *If you are, can you look back and give thanks for those people, situations, comments that had an impact on your life and helped your journey to start?*

3. *If the answer is, 'Not yet', what is it that would help you to get under way?*

4. *None of us can know when our journey will come to an end. But we can be sure that when we start that journey there is nothing that can separate us from the love of God in Christ Jesus (Rom. 8:39). Does that make you glad?*

Looking forward

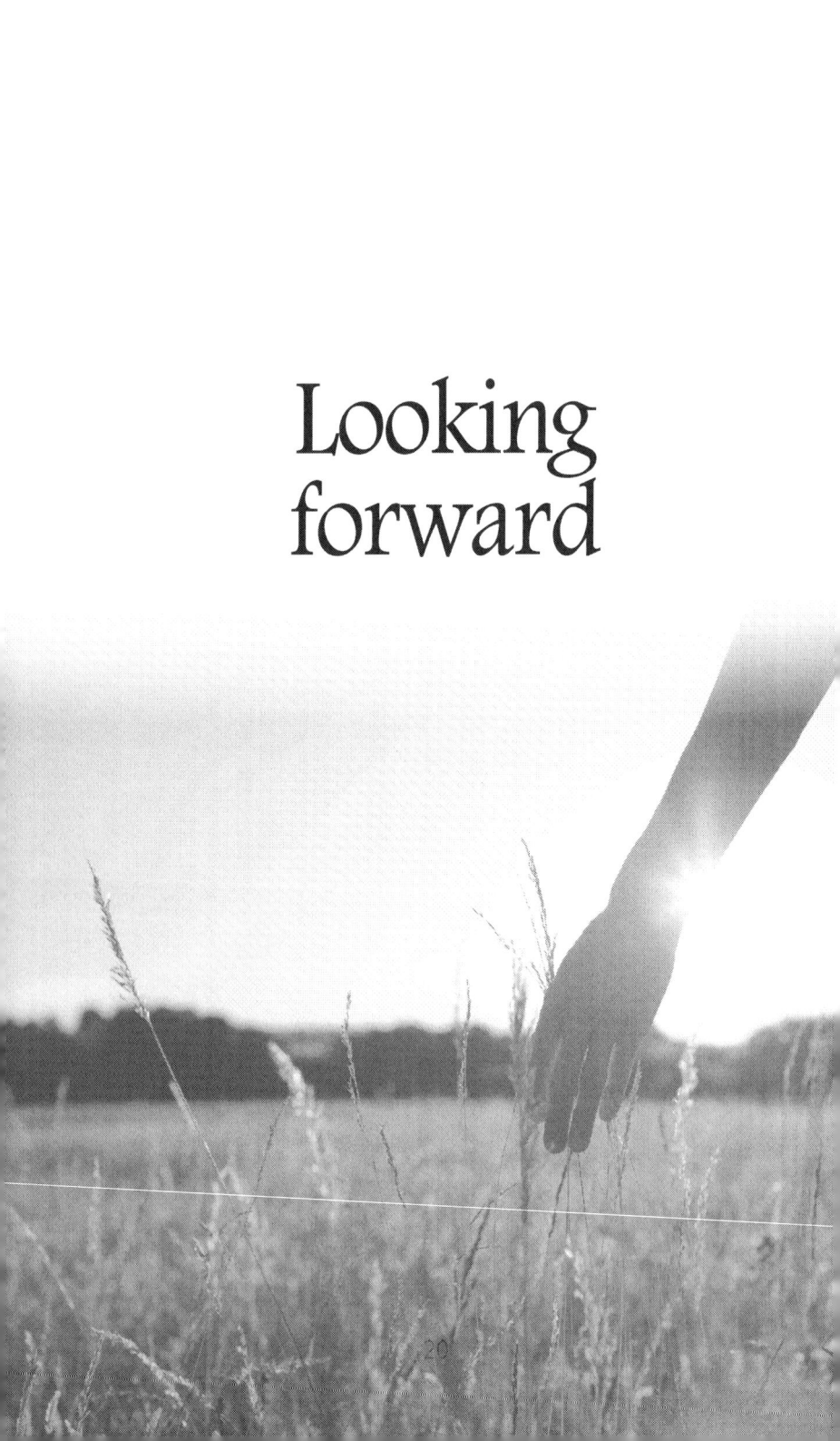

As young children, my brother and I spent a number of years growing up in Salisbury.

For those who do not know that city well, it used to be most famous for the city's Cathedral which, since 1549, has had the tallest spire of any church in England.[1] Sadly, the city became more well known in recent years following the use of a nerve agent in the attempted poisoning of a man (and his daughter) and the death of an unrelated local resident. However, it is the Cathedral and spire that hold iconic memories for me from my childhood.

I have visited the city from time to time as an adult and there is one point—travelling from the northeast—when you drive over the brow of a hill and there in front of you is a wonderful panorama with the Cathedral and its spire at the centre.

The first time I can remember driving that route as an adult and seeing what lay ahead produced a strong nostalgic reaction—it was unexpected but, to my eyes at least, something wonderful to behold.

Now, if ever I travel that way, I know what to expect but nevertheless it still stirs up thoughts and feelings: just looking at the simple image that lies ahead.

In the early 1990s, a film called *Shadowlands* was made of the story of C. S. Lewis' marriage and the death of his wife. At one point the two of them go looking for a valley (the Golden Valley) which they had seen in a painting hanging on the wall in Lewis' house.

In the film, that search is rewarded when they drive round a bend and there in front of them is the valley they had been searching for.[2]

Along the twisty Herefordshire roads in the film and also on the less windy road leading to Salisbury, one key quality that the car driver has to have is the ability to keep looking forward. As a child I could have told you about some of the things to be seen along the side of the road, for it was easier to look out of the side windows than over my parents' shoulders and out of the front windscreen. As a driver, being distracted by what is on either side of the road would, rightly, bring a rebuke or reminder from any passenger that I needed to 'Keep your eyes on the road.'

It is only by keeping looking ahead—keeping looking forward—that it is possible to catch the first glimpse of the skyline that promises the end of the journey, which means travellers going to the city are indeed nearly home.

For the people we read about in Psalm 126, there may well have been a sense of nostalgia for the very oldest among the travellers. They would have to have been in their seventies or even eighties if they were to have any real memory from their childhoods. My memories from early childhood are enhanced by photographs—obviously not available over 2,500 years ago! However, for others they had no memory of the city as such but they all, without exception, were overwhelmed at what lay ahead of them, like those who dreamed, mouths filled with laughter, singing with joy (vv. 1–2).

For all of them, this was much more than nostalgia—far more than reminiscences made real. Above all else, this had to do with promises fulfilled.

Promises

Daniel, at the beginning of a time of prayer recorded in Daniel 9, says that he 'understood from the Scriptures [referring to the Book of Jeremiah] … that the desolation of Jerusalem would last seventy years' (Dan. 9:2).

Zechariah asked God:

> How long will you withhold mercy from Jerusalem and from the towns of Judah, which you have been angry with these seventy years? (Zech. 1:12)

Why did Daniel pray and Zechariah ask questions of God? Why was seventy years mentioned by them both?

Perhaps it would be good to glance at a few things that God said would happen to the people of Judah. At this time, it would have been just the tribes of Judah and Benjamin and the Levites who were still in the land of Judah. God had spoken during the time when Babylon was the 'superpower' of the day and when they were replaced by the Persians.

For example, in the books of both Isaiah and Jeremiah:

- Conquest and captivity were coming (Jer. 25:8–9 and 40:1–3).

- But some of the people would return (Isa. 10:21; 44:24–26; 49:8–9 and Jer. 27:22).
- The period of exile would be seventy years (Jer. 25:11; 29:10).
- The return would usher in a new relationship with God (Isa. 61:4–6^3; 65:20–25).
- This would be utterly different from anything they had known before (Jer. 31:31–34).

There are many other promises that could be mentioned. Whether you just look at the ones quoted or choose to seek out and feast on yet others, there are just a few observations to be made:

- God knew what lay ahead for His people.
- God did not leave them in the dark. He revealed through His servants, like Isaiah and Jeremiah, what the future would hold.
- God had reasons for both the exile and the return.
- God's final purpose can be seen in verses found in Jeremiah 29: 'I know the plans I have for you, declares the Lord, plans … to give you hope and a future' (v. 11). But that was only true for those who would seek God with all their heart (Jer. 29:13).

The travellers in the Psalm had left their homes of captivity. They set out on a journey which most of them had never travelled before. They faced potential obstacles and difficulties on the way. Humanly speaking, they were doing it at the invitation of the Emperor of

Persia. But behind that human invitation they, perhaps with something of the insight of Daniel and Zechariah, recognized they were looking for God's promises to become a reality in their lives, in the days in which they lived, for them and their families.

When they saw the skyline of the City—when they walked through its gates and were able to wander around its streets, every step, every stone, every sound echoing their footfalls was an awesome reminder that God's promises had not failed—indeed that God's plans for them were most certainly to give them a future and a hope.

Not that the promises had yet reached their final wonder and glory. Isaiah, in particular, makes it clear that this will require New Heavens and a New Earth (Isa. 65:17). But the fact that they were able to see Jerusalem ahead of them and around them when they had entered the city, was clear, unquestionable and tangible evidence that God's promises were sure and certain and were surely and certainly coming true.

A modern song for children[4] has a chorus that says:

> We can be sure of this:
>
> God always keeps His promises.

I wonder what helps you to be sure of this.

Some years ago, I was asked to lead a time of 'Collective Worship' in one of the local schools near where we live.[5] The subject I was given was something like, 'The Cross as a Symbol of Christianity'. What thrilled me in my preparation was a time trawling the internet to find pictures of a variety of crosses, from those on tiny buildings in far flung parts of Africa, to old Celtic-shaped crosses in churchyards in the UK. It was clear that, with the possible exception of the Arctic and Antarctic, crosses were to be found on every continent in the world and the great majority of countries within those continents. Each one a reminder of God's promise that in heaven there will be those 'from every nation, tribe, people and language' (Rev. 7:9).

Perspective/priorities

Because the travellers trusted in God's promises—and were looking to see those promises fulfilled as they returned to Jerusalem—this gave them perspective in what was important and priorities in the choices that they made.

Remember that, if they had followed God's instructions through Jeremiah, they would have put down roots in the places where they had been taken into exile. God through Jeremiah had instructed them at the start of the seventy-year exile to:

> Build houses and settle down; plant gardens and eat what they produce. Marry and have sons and daughters; find wives for your sons and give your daughters in marriage, so that they too may have sons and daughters. Increase in number there; do not decrease. Also, seek the peace and prosperity

of the city to which I have carried you into exile (Jer. 29:5–7).

Each one of those things would have been like a strand within a rope, every strand making the rope stronger and thicker—each one tying them more closely to the place where they were living and making it harder to break away and start the journey back to Jerusalem.

The travellers, when they received the invitation from Cyrus, had to make a choice. Would they lay hold of the opportunity that the invitation afforded, or would they stay where they were, in the places that had become home and had been the focus of their prayers for peace and prosperity for nearly three quarters of a century?

What would help them make that choice?

Today we have almost the same choice. Now it is Christ who issues the invitation. At its simplest, it can be summed up as, 'Come to me,' or 'Follow me' (Matt 11:28; 9:9).

Like the people in Psalm 126, there are consequences that flow from accepting the invitation. J. C. Ryle in his book, *Holiness*, devotes a chapter to considering 'The Cost' (Luke 14:28).[6]

What helps us make the choice today?

One thing most certainly is the perspective that comes from looking to the end of the journey.

Paul tells us that nothing compares with the glory that will be revealed in us (Rom. 8:17–18).

Jesus, when showing His disciples the full extent of His

love, reminded them that He was going ahead to prepare a home for them, with Him, in His Father's house (John 13:1; 14:2–3).

Peter talks of the inheritance that 'can never perish, spoil or fade ... [which is] kept in heaven for you' (1 Peter 1:4).

As we look back through Christian history, there are many wonderful examples of those who lived lives with that sense of perspective and priority.

I had heard of David Livingstone when I was growing up. I knew that he was a great explorer and I also knew the story of his meeting with Henry Morton Stanley ('Dr Livingstone I presume'). What I did not know, because no one had told me, was the reason why Livingstone went to Africa and what motivated him to remain there despite all that happened to him and his family.

It was only later that I came to realize he was there as a child of God, seeking to take the good news ('the gospel') to those he had gone to serve. And part of that good news was to proclaim and promote freedom for captives and release for prisoners—especially for those trapped by the iniquitous practice of slavery (Isa. 61:1–2).

Reflecting on what motivated him he is quoted as saying:

> I place no value on anything I have or may possess, except in relation to the Kingdom of God. ... I shall most promote the glory of Him to whom I owe all my hopes in time or eternity.[7]

Perseverance

That sense of purpose, priority and perspective gave the travellers an ability to persevere.

Many had never seen the place they were going to. Almost none would know anything about the journey, how long it would take, what kind of terrain they would cross, what dangers there might be on the way, or indeed how their needs were to be supplied for the duration for the journey. And they would have had no real idea of what they were to expect when they arrived at the end of their journey.

Yet they made the choice to set out and, day by day and mile by mile, they continued on their way.

The Psalm tells us nothing of what happened to them on that journey. All that is clear is that they kept going and kept going until they reached their journey's end. In different generations, Christians have sung about our journey through life in the light of what lies ahead. For example:

- We're marching upwards to Zion the beautiful city of God.[8]
- Heaven's morning breaks, and earths vain shadows flee.[9]
- Our God is the end of the journey.[10]
- Before the Son we'll stand made faultless through the Lamb.[11]

Again and again, it is that focus on what lies at the end

of the journey which has allowed God's people to walk through every part of their life and we can say with the Psalmist, David:

> I will fear no evil, for you are with me;
> your rod and your staff, they comfort me.
> Surely your goodness and love will follow me all
>   the days of my life,
> and I will dwell in the house of the Lord forever
> (Ps. 23:4, 6).

Personal reflections

I used to meet with a Christian lady, who had originally moved into the local area to be an understairs maid in the 1920s. She loved nothing more than to talk of what lay ahead of her when she left her little flat for the home her Saviour was preparing for her in heaven. I am not sure how much blessing she received from my visits but I used to come away walking on air.

A week or so before writing this, I sang the hymn 'Standing on the Promises (of Christ my King)'[12]. It contains the statement that Christ is 'my all in all'. Is there a danger that at times I lose focus and take my eyes off Him and the home he is preparing for me in glory?

The Authorised King James Version translates Acts 17:6 as:

> These that have turned the world upside down are
> come hither also.

Christian history points us to many people who did 'turn the world upside down'.

It is often helpful to allow some time to pass to enable a clear-sighted view of any person's life and achievements to be formed. But, allowing for that, who are the people from the first quarter of the 21st century whose names, lives and service in God's hands will be added to those books of Christian history?

For reflection

1. *Are there things that are distracting you at present from looking forward? (Perhaps a more honest question would simply be to ask, 'What things are distracting you?' James 1:13 says 'when tempted' not 'if tempted').*

2. *What Bible passages, Christian books, songs or other things have helped you move forward or get back on track? I have had the opportunity of going back to things that were a help to me in years gone by—many of them have been a real tonic to my soul. Would it be helpful to go back to such things and refresh your heart, mind and soul?*

3. *God gives us many wonderful things in this life (see for example 1 Tim. 6:17 or Rom. 12:2). How easy do we find it to distinguish between the good, the better and the best?*

4. *What difference to your workplace or neighbourhood does your eternal perspective make?*

Looking
back

I well remember listening to a good friend of mine preaching about a meeting between Jesus and a leper.

One point that he made, forcefully and well, is that we are never told the name of any of the lepers that Jesus met. We are given no information about age, background, wealth or poverty, whether any of them had a family or were single people—we only know one thing about them: that they were lepers at the moment of their meeting with Jesus Christ.

And that is the same here in Psalm 126: we are simply told of their captivity. They were captives. The 'we' were people of captivity.

In other places in the Bible, we are given more information about the people who were taken away into captivity. There were kings, members of the royal family and nobility and priests, including the chief priest and his son. Among them were those who were good looking and intelligent (2 Chr. 36:5–6, 10; Dan. 1:3; Ezek. 1:3; 2 Kings 25:18; Ezra 7:1–7; Dan. 1:4). But, left behind, were the poorest people to work the vineyards and fields (2 Kings 25:12).

We can also see in other places more detailed information about those who returned from captivity, for example in Ezra 2 or Neh. 3. But in this Psalm, there are no names, no family backgrounds, no information about ages or position in society or indeed anything else about them.

We are simply told one thing: they had been captives—the city had been subject to captivity.

Where?

The Australian author, Graeme Goldsworthy, says that

> We see in the Bible the concept of the Kingdom of God as involving:
>
> God's people in
>
> God's place under
>
> God's rule.[1]

(I think I have seen as an addition, 'Knowing God's blessing'.)

For seventy years, two out of those three key facets and factors of God's Kingdom plan had not been in place.

They had been removed from God's place and taken to many, many different parts of the Babylonian Empire. A little later, looking at what had by then become the Persian Empire, Haman could say to the Emperor that the Jewish people had been 'dispersed and scattered among the people in all the provinces of [the] kingdom' (Esth. 3:8).

They had been removed from God's rule and placed under the rule and reign of the 'satraps, prefects, governors, advisors, treasurers, judges, magistrates and ... provincial officials' of the Empire of Babylon (Dan. 3:2)— in all the different parts of that Empire to which they had been taken. And above them all was an Emperor who, in a fit of rage, could condemn three men to be burned alive in a fiery furnace or slaughter a king's sons in front of their father's eyes and then blind that king so that the very last thing he ever saw was the death of those children (Dan. 3:19–20; 2 Kings 25:7).

In simple terms they were as far away from the place of God's Kingdom promise as they could possibly be and as distant from God's tender loving care as it was possible to imagine.

That state of affairs had lasted for seventy years.

We are told that patience is a virtue, but seventy years! In the oft quoted words of a famous tennis player, 'You cannot be serious!'

Why?

At any time in those seventy years, when there was a chance to reflect on the 'Why' of their being in that position, they had only to take hold of the Bible and look at the summaries given:

- Firstly, of the destruction of the Kingdom of Israel by the Assyrians—a lesson that the Kingdom of Judah simply ignored to their own peril (2 Kings 17:7–18).
- Then of their own situation (2 Kings 17:19–20; Jer. 3:6–10).

They had been taken away because they refused to listen to God—whether it was to take hold of the promises He had made or to heed the warnings He had given. In 2 Kings 17 the heart of the problem was that 'they would not listen ... they rejected His decrees ... they imitated the nations around them ...' (2 Kings 17:14–15).

Jesus Himself, reflecting on the people's history, said this:

> Jerusalem, Jerusalem, you who kill the prophets and stone those sent to you, how often I have longed to gather your children together, as a hen gathers her chicks under her wings, and you were not willing' (Luke 13:34).

They had only themselves, their hard hearts and their stubborn refusal to listen to blame. There was no one else at fault. It was utterly and unquestionably their responsibility. And for seventy long years they had had to suffer the consequences of that they had done.

Wow

But now: Wow!

The contrast was absolutely transformational. Their lives and the world in which they lived had been turned around.

No longer were they banished from God's place—it was that place that lay ahead of them.

Now they could look forward to being in God's place once again.

Above all else there was now the prospect of coming to

the place where God Himself was to be known, where He had said He would make His home and where His name was to be known (e.g., 2 Chr. 6:6).

No wonder they felt they must be dreaming, and their mouths were filled with joy. They knew only too well what it had been like living away from the place of God's loving care. Now they were returning, coming back to the place where they could know that love and that care as a present and daily reality in their lives. It was the contrast which enhanced that wonder—that made the overflowing joy so much more precious.

But what about us?

Where?

Where are we? Perhaps this needs to be a question for us both personally and also for the churches in whichever country we are living.

William Carey—who went himself to serve God in what is now India—in the introduction to his 'Inquiry into the Obligation of Christians to Use Means for the Conversion of' those not (yet) Christians said this:

> As our blessed Lord has required us to pray that His Kingdom may come, and His will be done on earth as it is in heaven, it becomes us not only to express our desires of that event by the word, but to use every lawful method to spread the knowledge of His name. In order to do this, it is necessary that we

should become in some measure acquainted with the religious state of the world.[2]

I could easily at this point turn into a grumpy old man. I could say:

> I have had a deep conviction for many years that practical holiness and entire self-consecration to God are not sufficiently attended to by modern Christians in this country. Politics, or controversy, or party-spirit, or worldliness, have eaten out the heart of lively piety in too many of us. The subject of personal godliness has fallen sadly into the background.

But, if I were to do so, I would be repeating part of the Introduction to the book, *Holiness by J. C. Ryle, written about 140 years ago.*[3] If you pick up Jane Austen's books from the early 1800s, they contain very unflattering but probably well-deserved pen portraits, or at least caricatures, of the clergymen of her day. The light which shone into the world of John Wesley and George Whitefield was against the backdrop of a woefully dark time for the Christian Church. If we were to go even further back in time to the days of Martin Luther and William Tyndale and Bishops Latimer and Ridley (whose deaths in the fire were, they hoped, to 'light a candle which would not go out'[4]) we would see that the Church of Jesus Christ has, at many times, faced dark and difficult days.

So, as we examine where we are, collectively and

personally, we need to be careful. We can be discouraged by the great distance that exists between our present position and where we might be in the fullness of God's 'good, pleasing and perfect will' (Rom. 12:2). But equally, let us never forget the times when God has stepped in to bring His Church and His people back closer to where He calls us to be.

Why?

The answer to the 'Why' question is going to be the same as the answer given about the peoples of Israel and Judah in 2 Kings 17.

We live after the coming of God's Son, Himself, into the world to be our Saviour. In the light of that historical certainty, we have even less of an excuse than they did (although 2 Kings 17 makes it very clear that they had no excuse at all).

Jesus told a parable in Matthew 21:33–41 about a landowner and his tenants who abused the land owner's servants. In the middle of that parable there is the line: 'They will respect my son … '(Matt. 21:37).

But of course, as the Gospel accounts make so clear, people did not respect Him when he was here on earth. And, unless people's lives and hearts and intentions are transformed by the regenerating work of God the Holy Spirit, that is the same today.

We refuse to listen to God; we are taught in many ways

to distrust the very certainty of God's existence; and we side-line the crucial significance of walking in His ways, both for this life and for eternity. And so, as in the days of the Judges, everyone does as they see fit (Judg. 17:6; 21:25).

As a result, we are cut off from God and strangers to His love and care.

Wow

But that is not how God has left us. It was never His intention to do so and through all of time, and even before time began, God planned to rescue rebels like you and me.

God did not stop at the planning stage. Among many other things, He is a 'completer finisher':

> The work which His goodness began,
> The arm of His strength will complete;
> His promise is Yea and Amen,
> And never was forfeited yet.[5]

The overwhelming wonder of this is that His plans, His purposes and His work are for rebels like you and me. God demonstrates His love in that while we were sinners Christ died for us, for Jesus Christ is the righteous one who died for the unrighteous (Rom. 5:8; 1 Peter 3:18).

J. C. Ryle reminds us:

> Many appear to forget that we are saved and justified as sinners, and only sinners; and that we never can attain to anything higher, if we live to

the age of Methuselah. Redeemed sinners, justified sinners, and renewed sinners doubtless we must be—but sinners, sinners, sinners, we shall be always to the very last.[6]

It was that wonder that Paul reflects on when writing to his protégé, Timothy (1 Tim. 1:15–16), that 'Christ Jesus came into the world to save sinners.' Truly that is a certainty which is worthy of full acceptance.

The apostle John was amazed at both the name that we now bear—God's children—and that this reflects the eternal reality of what God has done for us and in us. He had reminded his readers that we are all sinners but it is those same sinners, the 'we', who are now children of God (1 John 1:8; 3:1).

We need to stop and go, 'Wow!'—to spend some time worshipping God for His mercy and love, amazed by His goodness and His grace.

Personal reflection

I need to acknowledge that I can be drawn to look back to things that I enjoyed, things that still have an attraction to me. Temptations would not be what they were if they were not tempting. However, there is a clear instruction in Luke 17:32 to 'Remember Lot's wife!' John Bunyan in his book, *The Pilgrim's Progress*, devotes some time to a discussion between Christian and Hopeful on the significance of the 'old Monument' of a 'Woman transformed into the shape of a Pillar' that they encountered on their journey.[7]

That discussion does indeed take some time. In contrast, Christian, himself, at the very start of his journey, when people tried to persuade him to return to where he had come from, simply, 'put his fingers in his ears, and ran on, crying, "Life! Life! Eternal Life!"'[8]

When I look back is it always the reminder it should be, of how amazing it is that I have now escaped what would otherwise have been my fate?

An old hymn says:

> Oh to grace how great a debtor
> Daily I'm constrained to be![9]

Am I—honestly, truthfully—quite as regularly and consistently grateful to God for His grace in loving me and making that love real in my life? The hymn goes on:

> Let that grace, Lord, like a fetter,
> Bind my wand'ring heart to Thee.

Reflections

1. *Where have you come from? (Not just in terms of geography). What things in your life used to cut you off from knowing God and being one of His children?*

2. *How did God start the process of turning your life around? If there are specific people or events or circumstances, would it be good to thank God for the way He used them?*

3. *What things can make you look back in the wrong*

way—the way of Lot's wife? Have those things changed
over the years? How do you guard against them?

4. *What is the level of your 'Wow' factor as you look back*
to God's mercy in rescuing you and putting you on the
path to His heavenly home?

Can I stop for a moment and ask a different question? The
reflections in this chapter (and indeed other chapters in
this book) could be making an assumption that is not true
for every reader.

Cyrus issued an invitation to 'any of [God's] people' (2
Chr. 36:23). The efficiency of the Empire's bureaucracy
would have meant that everyone would have received
that invitation, but by no means did everyone accept that
invitation.

Jesus issued and continues to issue an invitation, which
is phrased in a number of different ways in the Bible. In
Romans 10, it is stated to be:

'Everyone who calls on the name of the Lord will be
saved' (v. 13),

'Anyone who trusts in Him will never be put to shame'
(v. 11).

Through the last 2,000 years, that invitation has been
heard and many multitudes of people have responded to
and accepted that call.

Are you among them?

If not, can I on His behalf ask you once again to call on

His name and to put your trust in Him so that you too, like Christian in *The Pilgrim's Progress*, receive the gift of eternal life.

A prayer that could be helpful for you to pray may be:

> Father in Heaven I know that there are things in my life, in my thoughts, words and actions, which mark me out as being in rebellion to your perfect will. I know that I do not have the power to turn my life back into your way. Please, through your Son, Jesus Christ, forgive me for the things that I have both done and failed to do that cut me off from you. Enable me to bow before you as my Lord and King and set my feet on the way that leads me to you and your heavenly home.

Look around

Chapter 4

How would you describe where you live?

During my working life, I spent time as a solicitor helping people move house. Over some forty years involved in that area of legal work, I read many descriptions of properties prepared by Estate Agents. Online you can find 'interpretation' tools to help you understand what is being said about a property, such as the following:

- *Bijou*—A tiny boxroom.
- *Cash buyers only*—No bank in its right mind would lend on this property.
- *Convenient for transport links*—Feel the walls shake as a train passes.
- *Cosy*—No more than one person per room at a time.
- *Close to good schools*—Can get there in ten minutes, if you [are a Formula 1 driver].
- *Easily maintained garden*—Concrete as far as the eye can see.
- *Full of history*—Does not have electricity or running water.
- *Perfect for a first-time buyer*—We know you cannot afford to be choosy.
- *Period property*—Derelict ...
- *Renovation required*—Watch money magically disappear.
- *Rural*—There is nothing there, except maybe some sheep.

- *Pied-à-terre*—Fancy French phrase for cosy.
- *Quirky*—Nothing matches and the doors are four-foot high.
- *Within walking distance*—If you have a spare five hours.
- *Sought-after area*—Ridiculous price.[1]

The Psalmist uses an image that needs interpreting when describing the land to which the travellers had returned: it was the reference to the Negev.

I know that some readers of this book may have been to the Negev themselves. If so, they can appreciate immediately what it is that the Psalmist meant. I have not been there myself but, on the morning that this chapter is being written, I read the start of the book of Judges as part of my daily time with God. In Chapter 1, v. 16 (ESV), there is a description of 'the wilderness of Judah which lies in the Negeb [Negev]'. This explains why, in the previous verse, Caleb's daughter asked her father 'also' for springs of water 'since you have given me land in the Negev' (Judg. 1:15; also Josh. 15:19).

Isaiah confirms the nature of the Negev as a land of hardship and distress (Isa. 30:6) and Britannica online describes the land as an 'arid region in the southern part of Israel and occupying almost half of Palestine west of the Jordan River ... The name is derived from the Hebrew verbal root ... "to dry" or "to wipe dry".'[2]

The Psalmist is looking around and being honest about

what the travellers saw. This was a land somewhere between a 'Period Property' and 'Renovation Required'. It was a land that, for seventy years, had received very little tender loving care, as the great majority of those who had reason to care had been carried away and barred from ever entering the land again.

They did not attempt to mask or hide the reality of their situation. They looked around and were honest with themselves and with what they could see.

But the very fact that they could see anything at all was because God was at work—because God's promises were in the process of being fulfilled.

An earlier generation, in the days of Samuel the Prophet, wanted to acknowledge that they were where they were because God had helped them. They marked their gratitude to God for his goodness at that point in time by setting up a marker stone, which they named 'Ebenezer'. That name is now more commonly associated with Scrooge in Charles Dickens' story, *A Christmas Carol*. But, in Samuel's days, it was not a person but a piece of rock to acknowledge, 'Thus far has the Lord helped us' (1 Samuel 7:12).

This was not the end of the story but a very clear and visible reminder that God had been with them and God had helped them to that point. And, of course, if He had done so 'thus far', there was every reason to expect Him to continue to do so in the days that lay ahead (1 Samuel 7:10–15).

The travellers knew that when they saw the Negev, they were looking into the land that God had promised to their ancestors—promises made in the days of Abraham, Isaac, Jacob (who became Israel) and their descendants; promises that had been repeated and reinforced both in the days of Moses, when the first of the tribes received land to settle in, and also through Joshua when the Negev itself became the possession of the tribe of Judah.

Then, as we have seen in an earlier chapter, God had promised to restore His people to the land of promise. And that is where they were and what they saw in front of their eyes.

But the promise was not yet completed. For, those promises through Isaiah and Jeremiah were for more than just a physical presence in the land. They were for a perfected relationship with God to be known in the land of God's promise.

This was neither a time for despondency as they were living in the days when God's promises were coming true, nor for complacency as the promises had much, much more yet to come to see their complete and perfect fulfilment.

So, what did they do?

Pray

Firstly, they prayed. There was, in their behaviour at this

point, an acknowledgement of what is said in the next Psalm:

Unless the Lord builds the house, its builders labour in vain (Ps. 127:1).

Their prayers recognized two things:

1. God's ability to transform the dry and barren land in which they found themselves into something that was refreshing and fruitful in God's hands. It would be interesting to know if they had in their minds some of the promises God makes, in Isaiah 35, when they called out to God in the way that they did in v. 4. Certainly, the imagery of people on a journey and, also, water in the desert and the transformation that water will bring, is very clear in, for example, Isa. 35:8 and also vv. 1–2, 6–7. The result is seen in Isa. 35:3:

> Strengthen the feeble hands,
>
> Steady the knees that give way;

2. God's stated purposes for His people. Perhaps the best-known promise which declares those purposes is in Jer. 29:11–14. God states clearly that His goal for His people is to give them a future and a hope. What the people saw at the time of their arrival in the land was not the fullness of those promises; for that to become true more was to follow and they were praying in the assurance that what God had said, He would bring to pass. The

English Standard Version and the New American
Standard Bible translate the start of Jer. 29:14:

I will be found by you, declares the Lord, and
I will restore your fortunes.

The same is said in Jer. 30:18[3] and, again in the
ESV and NASB, in Jer. 30:3. God's people are praying
God's promises into their situation. And we can see
more of the energizing reliance on God's promises
in the prayers of two of God's great Old Testament
champions in Dan. 9:4–19 and Neh. 1:5–11.

Their prayer does not limit God by telling Him how He
should restore their fortunes.

However, they do take one of His promises, clearly and
directly, and use that as the bedrock for their praying.
The only thing they add is their trust that, when God does
act, it will be a good thing. For when streams flow in the
Negev they bring life and fruitfulness; they turn an arid
and dry place into a place that demonstrates another of
God's promises come to fruition. This is found in Isaiah
41:18–20, where God promises to make rivers flow on
barren heights and that the desert will grow cedar, acacia,
myrtle, olive, pines, fir and cypress. These are pictures
both of plenty and also of a long-term change—not just a
short-term crop or flowering but long enough for trees to
grow and flourish.

William Carey took lines from the Lord's Prayer—that
His Kingdom would come and His will would be done on

earth—as the starting point for His 'Inquiry'. Many of us have spent many years praying the words of that prayer, some as part of our regular weekly services—the older among us may even remember saying it as part of school assemblies when we were children.

Do we pray that God would answer that prayer for the street where our home is to be found, our place of work, our neighbourhood, the village, town or city where we live? How will that street, workplace, neighbourhood and so on change when God does indeed make His Kingdom come and His will be done there?

Clearly that will involve people coming into God's Kingdom as His children. But what else may it or should it mean for the community in which we live and, for some, in which we work?

Practice

Prayer is not all that they did.

They were looking around. They recognized what was needed and they acted accordingly.

The land God had promised to His people was a land of great potential. It was described in the days of Moses as a land flowing with milk and honey. That description is given by God to Moses at their first meeting when God made Himself known in a burning bush (Exod. 3:4, 8). And that description of the Land of Promise is used again and again throughout the journey from slavery in Egypt to the entry into the Land itself (e.g., Exod. 13:5; 33:3; Lev. 20:24; Num. 13:27). The last of those references has moved from being an image of something that had yet to be seen to a description of what Joshua, Caleb and the other members of the reconnaissance party had actually seen for themselves: 'It does flow with milk and honey.' As evidence of this plenty, they brought back a cluster of grapes that required two men to carry it.

The nature of the land and its potential to provide plenty for them to enjoy had not diminished. But for seventy years the land had been neglected. The second book of Chronicles 36:21 describes it as a period of 'sabbath rests' and a time of 'desolation'. When the people returned, the thorns, weeds and other evidence of land lying fallow for that length of time must have been obvious for them to see.

And so, they set about making changes. They set about doing what was needed in the land. They took seed and sowed it. But, for that seed to germinate and bear fruit, there must have been day after day of hard, back-breaking toil to prepare the ground, clear the weeds and give space for the plants that they had sown to grow and bear fruit.

The key was that they were working towards changing what so clearly needed to be changed.

We could consider a number of things that they did not do. But God does not bring those to our attention. What He does is tell us clearly what they did do.

They looked and saw what was needed and they focused their efforts and their abilities on meeting those needs.

And in doing so we see, once again, God's promises being fulfilled.

God's Kingdom promise to Abraham was that he would be blessed and also that he would be a blessing—indeed that all the peoples on earth would be blessed through him (Gen. 12:2–3).

Psalm 126:5–6 shows something of that blessing. Twice we are told that the people—those who had started in a dry and arid place—would sing songs of joy. And in each case, it is directly the fruit of their work which is the reason for their joy. Sowing leads to reaping and seed is turned into sheaves of the crop they had sown.

Personal reflection

I am sure that there are many aspects of the travellers' prayer that I need to hold on to more clearly, including:

- Does prayer come first? Or is there a risk that I have ideas and even start turning them into plans before I seek to know God's will?
- How often do I take hold of God's promises to help me frame my prayers when I come to Him?
- Do I have the audacity to think I know how God may or will answer my prayers and the prayers of others?[4]
- I quite often find myself thinking in pictures

or images. How can I distinguish between my sanctified thought processes and those which are just my own ideas?

How well do I recognize what the true needs are for the community in which I live? I was very privileged to get to know a very dedicated and committed area officer, working for our local authority in the communities around our church. She was able to give me an understanding of local needs that I would have found much harder to know without her help. She retired a little while ago and I miss that contact and the insights she was able to provide.

Reflections

1. *Is your personal life dry or arid? What about the life and work of the church of which you are part? An old song makes a distinction between times of 'mercy drops' and of 'showers of blessing'.[5] The hymn's first line says, 'There shall be showers of blessing.' When will that be for you and for the place God has called you to work?*

2. *What changes would there be for you, your family, your church and your community if God were to restore your fortunes?*

3. *What are the needs in your neighbourhood? What steps could you take to gain a better understanding of your community?*

4. *What is it that God's people could be doing to change the local communities where we each live so that they*

are increasingly places where God's Kingdom comes and His will is done?

INTRODUCTION TO PART 2

I had heard a phrase used many times but had no idea where it came from until I checked for the purpose of writing this part of this book. The phrase is:

> The Lord hath yet more light and truth
> To break forth from His Word.[1]

I hope I will not offend anyone who loves the hymn but I probably would not choose to count it as one of my most favourite songs. However, the statement in the two lines quoted is absolutely correct.

The great Victorian preacher, C. H. Spurgeon, recognizing the inexhaustible nature of God's supply that is to be found in the Bible, said:

> If when I get to heaven the Lord shall say to me, 'Spurgeon, I want you to preach for all eternity,' I would reply, 'Lord, give me a Bible, that is all I need.'[2]

Knowing how little I have so far found of that inexhaustible supply is one reason that I, along with many other people, read the Bible from cover to cover and then start again and intend, as God enables me, to continue in that pattern. I was first challenged to read the Bible that way by a friend in my student days and it has been my normal pattern of Bible reading for over forty years.

Others find different methods more helpful and it is important that each of us find ways that help us to keep on looking into God's Word—all of it—expecting to receive more light and more truth in everything we read. Paul told Timothy that all Scripture is 'profitable' (Authorised King James Version of 2 Tim. 3:16). Do we expect to profit from reading God's Word every day or every time we do so?

It could be that there is a particular danger for preachers. When you have spent time in studying a passage from God's Word and, with God's help, moulded that study into a form that can be preached, you know that you can only shine the light onto a few signposts for others to see. By God's grace, those signposts will be a blessing to the hearers and equip people for the good work that God has for them to do (2 Tim. 3:17). But, once that set of signposts has been identified, it can be hard to go back to the passage and see it with fresh eyes.

Over the next three chapters, we are going back to Psalm 126 to look again at the same part of God's Word, set in the same context of God's promises being fulfilled, but with a different set of signposts to show the way. This second set of signposts are not the only other ones that could be found.

Eyes

Every summer for many years my wife's family used to travel down to the beautiful Dorset town of Lyme Regis. One of the challenges on that journey was to be the first person to see the sea. It is quite some distance before the journey reaches its end. On a good day, the sea can be seen from the hills between places called Winterbourne Abbas and Bridport. However, that stretch of the road is also prone to low lying cloud that can obscure the view. Whether or not it could be seen, however, the sea was still there! It had not changed and it had not gone away, whatever the eyes of drivers and passengers on the road could actually see themselves.[1]

The travellers In Psalm 126 used their eyes and it is the response to what they saw that is recorded in v. 1 and the first half of v. 2.

You would think that what they saw would have had to have been beautiful and glorious—a sight as close to perfection as it is possible to see in this world. In fact, of course, this Psalm does not actually tell us what the City did look like when they saw it.

But, in the Book of Nehemiah, we get a partial description:

- Firstly, in 1:3, Nehemiah is told that, 'The wall of Jerusalem is broken down and its gates have been burned by fire.'
- Then, during his inspection (2:13–15), among

other things, the same assessment of the walls and gates is repeated.

- He reports back his observations to those in the City (2:17), where Jerusalem as a whole and not just the walls is described as being in ruins.
- In a mockery of the work (4:3), the walls are seen as being so weak that a fox climbing on them would bring them tumbling down.

Near where we live, around the old heart of Southampton, you can walk around the City's old walls. Many significant parts of those walls were destroyed by bombing during WWII. They are interesting as a monument to days gone by but useless for their original purpose of providing a defence for the city and its inhabitants. They are now no more than a historical curio, of no use for people in today's world.

Yet, when the travellers saw those broken-down walls—when they saw into the ruins of the city—what they saw with their eyes produced an immediate and amazed reaction. The dream is not a nightmare, it is a 'pinch me: am I awake?' type dream—for what they see, through their eyes, is unbelievably wonderful. That is why their mouths are filled with laughter.

What are they seeing?

I would like to suggest that it was not the fire-damaged gates or the ruined walls that caused the reaction that came from their lips. It was what those gates and walls represented—what they meant to the people that saw them.

For, those gates and walls, however damaged and defaced, were a reminder of God's promises and an assurance that those promises were being fulfilled in their day and for them as God's people.

As we saw in Chapter 2 of this book that God's promises talked of a sequence of interlinked events which included:

- A period of captivity and exile—by the time the Psalm was written that had happened.
- The period of exile would be seventy years.
- Some of the people would return. The timing means that this must be what the journey is actually about.
- The return would usher in a new relationship with God—not yet, not quite yet … how soon …
- This would be utterly different from anything they had known before. Oh, the sense of expectancy and anticipation!

But to see things in this way you have to see what has happened, is happening and will happen through a lens. It is a lens of God—God's sovereign control of His world and of His promises being both believable and believed.

Many years ago, I read in a science fiction book a comment on a particular sculpture by Auguste Rodin[2]. The book is not one I would choose to read again but the image of the sculpture and the comment itself have remained with me:

> Anybody can look at a pretty girl and see a pretty girl. An artist can look at a pretty girl and see the old woman she will become. A better artist can look at an old woman and see the pretty girl that she used to be. But a great artist—a master—and that is what Auguste Rodin was—can look at an old woman, portray her exactly as she is ... and force the viewer to see the pretty girl she used to be.[3]

Did the travellers each need to be great artists to be able to see beyond the fire-damaged gates and the ruined walls to the promise-enriched reality that they revealed?

I am so glad that it did not need great artistic skill or a master's eye as, otherwise, I would have been shut out from any understanding or appreciation of what they saw[4]. No, all that was needed was for them to take hold of God's promises, acknowledge them for what they were and look at the world through the lens of those promises.

I wonder how many, including many who are part of Bible-believing churches, try looking at things through the wrong end of the telescope. In practical terms, we can look at God's promises through the lens of our experiences in the world, rather than the correct way round.

By using the right viewpoint, the travellers found laughter and joy. The wrong way round is likely to lead to despondency and despair.

What promises?

An old song speaks of those who are standing on the promises of Christ [their] king.[5]

But which promises?[6]

In 1859, 'The Great Blondin' was the first man to walk across the Niagara Falls gorge on a tightrope. He started on the United States side.[7] There were various things that happened on the way during his different attempts. However, for any of them to be successful first things had to come first. And the most important of all was that the rope had to be securely fastened at the other end of his journey. The end of his journey had to be marked and secured in Canada, on the Canadian side of the falls.

And for us too—the promises of God are clearly marked at the end of the journey. Many people would say that the best-known verse in the Bible, which includes one of the most wonderful promises in the Bible, is John 3:16—God's promise of eternal life to those who believe in God's one and only Son.

This is developed in John 5:24 with a past, a present and a future:

- Past—has crossed from death to life.
- Present—has eternal life.
- Future—will not be condemned.

And in that future, there is a home being prepared for us by God's Son, Himself. It will be a place where there will be no more death, mourning, crying or pain and ' in which righteousness dwells' (John 14:2–3, Rev. 21:4; 2 Peter 3:13). For those who have stood at the side of an open grave or sat in a crematorium waiting for the curtains to close, or for others who have been beside a person we loved at the very moment of death, then we know in special measure just how precious and indeed crucial those promises are. For Paul is very clear that if God's promises do not give the answer to death, then we might as well pack up our bags and go home (1 Cor 15:16–19). It is at this point that Paul uses that wonderful word, 'But'. The greatest assurance is the actual resurrection of Jesus, Himself—His own personal triumph over death (1 Cor 15:20–24) and so Paul can say in 1 Cor 15:57:

> But thanks be to God! He gives us the victory through our Lord Jesus Christ.

First Steps

It may have struck you that the Niagara Falls illustration was a bit one sided. For not only was it important to have the rope fixed at the end of the journey (in Canada), but it was just as important to have it fixed at the start of the journey in the USA.

When we set off on our journey the promises are a crucial starting point. That starting point has its bedrock in eternity and its history on a hillside outside the city of Jerusalem:

> At Calvary's cross is where you begin
>
> When you come as a sinner to Jesus.[8]

It was on the cross that Jesus exchanged our sin for His righteousness by taking the punishment for our sin into Himself and, in return, giving us spotless new robes (Zech. 3:3–4; Rev. 7:9). It was at the cross that He faced death for us so that we might know eternal life.

And God makes promises to all who put their trust in Him; who believe in Him; who call on His name; to all who receive from God the gift of faith (Rom. 10:11; Acts 16:31; Rom. 10:13, Eph. 2:8).

Those initial promises often include the words *have* or *are*:

- We *are* children of God—1 John 3:1.
- We *have* eternal life or simply life—John 3:16; 20:31.
- We *have been* cleansed—2 Peter 1:9; Eph. 5:26.
- Our sins *have been* forgiven—1 John 2:12 and Luke 5:20, 23.
- We *have been* saved and made alive—Eph. 2:5, 8.
- We *are* new creations in Christ, the old gone and the new come—2 Cor. 5:17.

How many times could we add more to that list? We will only scratch the surface of all the wonderful changes that God has already done for those who have become His people in Jesus Christ.

Just before we move on, I have been reminded that a

good number of these promises are like Blondin's tight rope. They stretch from the start of the journey to the end. That is especially true of John 3:16. It is a reminder that eternal life is a present experience.

Many years ago, I remember a young lady who was attending a conference of a fairly sober and serious group of Christians. She knew that eternal life was one of God's promises to those who trusted in Jesus Christ. However, she thought of it purely and exclusively in terms of what would happen to her when she died. During the course of that conference, some wise and godly people helped her to realize that she had, in the present, eternal life and it was not limited in the way she had thought. They probably did not know the effect it would have on her. She was seen doing cartwheels in the grounds of the place they were staying, so great was her wonder and joy at God's present gift of eternal life.

On the way

God's promises are not just for the start and the end of the journey. There are many that are for us on the way.

Some are constant. For example, God promised His people that He would never leave them and never forsake them (Deut. 31:6 and Hebrews 13:5), and He has also told us that nothing can separate us from His love in Christ (Rom. 8:39).

Some are developmental. So, God's people are those

who are being transformed into [the Lord's] likeness with ever increasing glory—this being the work of God the Holy Spirit who sanctifies us and who demonstrates His transforming work in the form of fruit growing in our lives (2 Cor. 3:18, Rom. 15:16 and Gal. 5:22–23). Some of these can be seen as commands but those commands are part of God's perfect will for us on the journey, not just at journey's end. For example, we are to keep in step with God the Holy Spirit since we live by the Spirit (Gal. 5:25) and to grow up into Christ (Eph. 4:15).

Some of God's promises come fully and gloriously formed from Him and Him alone:

- Jesus promised that He would be with His disciples always, to the very end of the age (Matt 28:20).
- Paul prayed that his readers in Ephesus would be enlightened to know the power of God for them, the same power that raised Jesus from the dead (Eph. 1:18–20).

Yet other promises call on us to be involved, perhaps most clearly in Phil. 2:12–13, where we are commanded to work out our salvation because it is God who is at work in us.

These are just a tiny selection. But hopefully, they will produce a similar response to that of the travellers in the Psalm. Their response was laughter and songs of joy.

Looking/lens

The travellers looked at the walls and gates of Jerusalem and saw God's promises being fulfilled.

What are the things that help us to see afresh—to see with wonder and worship both the reality of God's promises and the certainty that they are being fulfilled in our day, in the circumstances that we find ourselves in, whatever and wherever that might be?

Personal reflection

At the time of writing, a friend of mine has been living in a place of significant danger and worry for the last few weeks. He has been encouraging his family and his church to read the Bible and trust in God. In particular, he has been encouraging them to look at Psalm 91. His ten-year-old son was found reading the Bible at midnight when he found it difficult to sleep, to help him 'not fear the terror of night', for God promises to cover [him] with His feathers and under His wings he can find refuge (Ps. 91:5, 4).

Reflection

1. *What promises of God are most important to you? How did they first find you out? Are there any steps you could take to refresh them in your heart and soul?*

2. *Are there things happening to you or that you see happening in the world around that are like fire-damaged gates or broken defences in your mind's eye?*

3. *Are there people you can turn to, songs that you can*

sing (or indeed anything else), that may help you to see things through the lens of God's promises?

4. *The second book of Corinthians 1:20 says that no matter how many promises God has made, they are 'Yes' in Christ. Yes? Do all God's people say 'Amen'?*

Ears

D o you ever read a Bible passage and ask, 'I wonder why it says things in that particular way?'

I certainly find myself doing that when it comes to the second half of verse 2 and on into verse 3 in Psalm 126:

> Then it was said among the nations, 'The Lord has done great things for them.'
>
> The Lord has done great things for us, and we are filled with joy.

Why is it that the acknowledgement of God's goodness is first 'among the nations'? Why not?

> Then it was said among God's people …
>
> Then we said one to another …
>
> Then we were reminded from God's Word …

In this chapter we will look at two possible explanations. One or perhaps even both may be your experience of what has happened in your life and through you to others.

It may say something about my way of thinking and my recent experiences as to which one of the two we will look at first.

Forgettery

To see just how significant the place of 'the nations' was, we need to go back from Psalm 126 to a command issued by Cyrus, as it is recorded in Ezra Ch 1.

This command was that the travellers were to be provided with silver and gold, with goods and livestock and with freewill offerings for God's Temple in Jerusalem.

This generous provision was to be made by the 'people of any place where' the travellers had been living (v. 4).

From this, we can see what it is that those nations would have seen. It would have been a group of returning refugees. However, the command issued by Cyrus marks a real difference to what might, more normally, be our expectation or our imagery of refugees.

This would not have been a line of downtrodden, emaciated men and women with their families, stumbling back to their long-abandoned homes. These were travellers, granted freedom to travel by the Emperor, himself, with a clear purpose to their journey and with all that they would need provided by the people among whom they had lived for the last seventy years. It is the nations— the nations spoken about in Psalm 126—who had been the ones called on by Cyrus to make those provisions available from their own resources for the people of God.

Truly God had done great things in granting release from captivity, freedom to travel and all that was needed to enable them to do God's work in Jerusalem (Ezra 1:2–4).

The nations helped them and then, even greater provision came when the looted Temple articles were handed back for the travellers to take with them (Ezra 1:6–8).

Over the last few years, it has been my privilege to be able to visit about ten or so churches in the southeast of England reasonably regularly. Most are within a relatively short distance of where I live. Most of those visits have been as the 'visiting speaker / preacher'.

I have also had an opportunity to get to know leaders and members of other local churches.

It would be fair to say that most of the churches I have come to know are small in their numbers. That can change in God's goodness and one church I know has increased in size by nearly ten times.

Often at the end of a time together, I will find myself talking to someone from the church and ask or hear about what is happening among God's people. Not always, but reasonably often, this can be put in terms of what is not happening rather than what is. One church's website had a headline that said, 'We don't have a Pastor at present.' This was true but not a very encouraging introduction to the church. Others have told me that they do not have a Sunday School, that they have had to close a particular activity or that they long to run a youth club, even when they are living in an area which is largely for retired people and they are doing a great work among the older generation.

As a visitor or outsider, it is sometimes easier to note and comment on the things that are actually happening. It may be a level of fellowship and care—the way in which a tiny church puts in a lot of time and effort to support a nearby Food Bank and at the same time opens up its building to local people who come in for coffee. It may also be the way that a church, with a vision for God's Kingdom, shares its resources of time and people to support work that is going on in a local school, even though it is other local churches who see the fruit of that work in their children's club or young people's group. Yet others knit *Teddies 4 Tragedies*[1] for use in caring for children who have lost their homes in the Middle East; host a time to welcome adults with learning difficulties; or host a time with workers from both their own and other churches.

When you are in the middle of a situation, it is sometimes hard to see beyond the things that are tricky or difficult. We sometimes speak of seeing the light at the end of the tunnel but, in some situations, there are still too many twists and turns ahead for any light to be seen easily from inside that particular tunnel.

Alongside that reality is the risk that, as Christians, particularly those who have been Christians for a long time, we can forget just how different life in the church can be from life in the world outside the church.

I remember a lady who started attending church having had her first contact through our 'Mothers & Toddlers' Group. When she came to the church, the one thing she found hard to get over was the way in which young and old got on with, cared for and showed love for each other. In particular there were two ladies, one eighty years old and the other eighteen, who in so many ways were different from each other but who demonstrated real love and care for each other.

I hope that many people reading this, who themselves have been in churches for a number of years, will be wondering why I have mentioned this example. There are, I hope, many examples that we could each pick out in our own experience, both from the church we are part of now and from other churches that we have been part of in days gone by. It is what you would expect; it is what ought to be the case among those who are part of God's redeemed family.

But we live in a culture and a society that is splintered and divided in so many ways.

We expect other Christians to believe in the wonder of God's grace to us and also to practice grace in our dealings with one another. We are God's forgiven people and we should also demonstrate that we are God's forgiving people, because we know that, in Christ, we are part of a family made up of people of every nation, tribe, people and language.

Not that any church totally gets it right. As has been said, 'If you find the perfect church, don't join it: you'd spoil it.'[2]

And we do not always see things as we should. C. S. Lewis has a wonderful description of a church as we might see it, in his book, *The Screwtape Letters*, which were written in 1942 from the point of view of a devil tempting a human being:

> One of our great allies at present is the Church itself. Do not misunderstand me. I do not mean the Church as we see her spread out through all time and space and rooted in eternity, terrible as an army with banners. That, I confess, is a spectacle which makes our boldest tempters uneasy. But fortunately, it is quite invisible to these humans. All your patient sees is the half-finished, sham Gothic erection on the new building estate. When he goes inside, he sees the local grocer with rather an oily expression on his face bustling up to offer him one shiny little book containing a liturgy which neither of them understands, and one shabby little book containing corrupt texts of a number of religious lyrics, mostly bad, and in very small print. When he gets to his pew and looks round him, he sees just that selection of his neighbours whom he has hitherto avoided. You want to lean pretty heavily on those neighbours. Make his mind flit to and fro between an expression like 'the body of Christ' and the actual faces in the next pew ...[3]

Are we told that it was 'said among the nations' because the nations could see something that God's people had forgotten? Could it be that the people of God had become so familiar with the fact that God was working in them and for them, that they were no longer amazed by what it was that God was doing?

This may be just for me—but are there times when I need to remind myself, or I need other people to help to remind me, just how grateful and thankful I should be to God for His love, His grace and His mercy to me?

Overflow

Psalm 126 can be read as a direct movement from the first part of v. 2 into the second half of the verse. On this basis, it would be that by the laughter and joy of the people, that resounded in an echo in the nations around, the people of the nations heard what God had done and the only way they could respond was in their own acknowledgment of God's goodness and the great things He had done.

Cyrus' command (in Ezra 1) would have been unexpected if the people had not remembered and recognized the promises that God had made those seventy years beforehand. The fact that they did remember is acknowledged in Ezra 1:1. For it is God who brought back the people and not Cyrus who sent them back. God had not only arranged the events of history to enable them to return but had also fulfilled a much earlier promise not to leave or forsake them (Deut. 31:6). He was with them from the start of the journey to the end. And so, their rejoicing was an outward expression of their gratitude to God for what He had done, was doing and would continue to do.

The nations must have heard about the wonder of the journey as the travellers made their way from the far-flung corners of the, now, Persian Empire. People coming from 'any place' (Ezra 1:4) that they had lived but converging on one place—Jerusalem.

As they travelled along, there would have been questions about the laughter and joy; questions about why they were carrying so much gold and silver; people disturbed by cattle lowing and sheep bleating. 'What', 'why', 'where', 'how did this happen?' Questions which would have been asked again and again on the journey and always the same response—perhaps like the following:

> The LORD has done this, and it is marvellous in our eyes. The LORD has done it this very day; let us rejoice today and be glad (Ps. 118:23–24, NIV 2011 translation).

And then the people echoed back what the nations around said in Psalm 126:3.

I was not brought up in the countryside or know how to lay a log fire in an open hearth. I still remember the person who first showed me how to do it. I was told that to get the fire going well you need to have two logs both alight lying next to each other, so that the heat in one is reflected back and increased by the heat in the other. The wonder of the people was echoed by those around who saw it and that, in turn, further fuelled the people's gratitude and expressions of thanks to God.

It was a virtuous spiral of recognition, thanks, praise and then further recognition, thanks, praise ...

Personal reflection

I wonder how often, for example at work, people would look at me and see joy as the most evident quality in my life. One of the downsides when preaching on video conferencing networks is that you cannot help looking yourself in the eye. How clearly is appreciation and wonder at what God has done evident in the person who looks back at me?

In 2 Kings 7, there is the story of the siege of Samaria. When the siege was lifted, by God doing a great thing, the first people to realize were a group of four lepers. They had a debate as to what they should do. Were they to keep the good news to themselves or tell the people in the city, who were unaware of what God had done? Their conclusion was this: 'We're not doing right. This is a day of good news and we are keeping it to ourselves' (2 Kings 7:9).

Is there any danger that I am keeping the good news of God's great things to myself?

Reflection

1. *If you were to ask your neighbours about the great things God has done, how would they respond?*

2. *Thinking about the place(s) God has placed you— home, neighbourhood, work, church—what has God*

done over the last twelve months and how much do you want to thank Him for those good things?

3. *We are not yet at the end of the journey. What more has God yet to do in your life, in your community?*

4. *How can you encourage yourself in remembering the great things God has done?*

5. *Which people have you found that encourage you? How did they do that? Who can you encourage, yourself, and how?*

Emotions

If verse 1 and the first part of verse 2 are about what they saw with their eyes and the second part of verse 2 and verse 3 about what they heard with their ears, then there is one thing that is true about the whole Psalm: it is about their emotions.

- v. 1—Feeling as if the travellers were dreaming.
- v. 2—Laughter and joy.
- v. 3—Filled with joy.
- v. 5—Tears and joy.
- v. 6—Weeping and joy.

And in verse 4 there is a clear sense of hope—hope that their cry to God will be heard and that the God who had, already, done great things for them would continue in the same vein in answering those prayers.

It would be wrong to say that the Psalm encompasses a whole gamut of emotions. However, it does cover a wide range of possible emotions as the travellers look back, look forward and look around at the situation they find themselves in.

Motive

Some fifty years ago, Evangelical Press published a series under the title, 'Pastoral Booklets'.[1] Among them is one where the writer wanted to help his readers understand what had not only motivated the apostle Paul but also enabled him to keep on and on serving God in the way that he did.[2]

Paul did not have an easy time in his life as a follower of Jesus Christ. At one point he talks of 'light and momentary troubles' (2 Cor 4:17), but as you read on in that letter, he very reluctantly gives an idea of what those troubles actually were. He had:

> ... been in prison more frequently, been flogged more severely, and been exposed to death again and again. Five times I received from the Jews the forty lashes minus one. Three times I was beaten with rods, once I was pelted with stones, three times I was shipwrecked, I spent a night and a day in the open sea, I have been constantly on the move. I have been in danger from rivers, in danger from bandits, in danger from my fellow Jews, in danger from Gentiles; in danger in the city, in danger in the country, in danger at sea; and in danger from false believers. I have laboured and toiled and have often gone without sleep; I have known hunger and thirst and have often gone without food; I have been cold and naked. Besides everything else, I face daily the pressure of my concern for all the churches (2 Cor. 11:23–28).

I think I would find it very hard to consider those things either momentary or light!

What was it that enabled Paul to keep on keeping on?

Most definitely it was not seen by the preacher as a response to the poster saying, 'Keep Calm and Carry On'.

That poster was designed some ninety years after the sermon that forms the booklet was preached.

M'Cheyne acknowledges that Paul was, by his nature, an active man. Today we might call him an activist. But he then argues it was more than his natural ability or natural tendencies that kept him keeping on.

Sometimes we can try and encourage ourselves or challenge each other by a sense of duty—by looking to the things we ought to do. That can take us some distance but there comes a point where our sense of duty will give up and take us no further. Indeed, it can easily descend into a motivation by guilt.

For some people we may feel a sense of gratitude and a desire to pay back what we owe to those who have helped us. But even here there is a point beyond which gratitude will not take us.

M'Cheyne points us to the greatest, the most wonderful and the most powerful motive in the whole universe. His sermon was, like the two references already made in this chapter, from 2 Corinthians. There, in 2 Cor. 5:14, Paul says that 'Christ's love compels us.'[3]

He demonstrates that this is first and foremost Christ's love for us and not the other way around. Then he goes on to show that it was this love which enabled Paul to be constant and consistent in following and serving his Saviour:

As the natural sun in the heavens exercises a

mighty and unceasing attractive energy on the planets which circle round it, so did the Sun of Righteousness, which had indeed arisen on Paul with a brightness above that of noon-day, exercise on his mind a continual and an almighty energy, constraining him to live henceforth no more unto himself, but to Him that died for him and rose again. And observe, that it was no temporary, fitful energy, which it exerted over his heart, and life, but an abiding and a continued attraction; for he doth not say that the love of Christ did once constrain him; or that it shall yet constrain him; or that in times of excitement, in seasons of prayer, or peculiar devotion, the love of Christ was wont to constrain him; but he saith simply, that the love of Christ constraineth him. It is the ever-present, ever-abiding, evermoving power, which forms the main-spring of all his worlding; so that, take that away, and his energies are gone, and Paul is become weak as other men.[4]

Love part 1

All God's dealings with His people were on the basis of love. For example, in Deut. 7:7–8, Moses reminded the people that God had set his affection on them and chosen them, not because of their number but because He loved them. He goes on to promise a covenant of love for a thousand generations (Deut. 7:9). And then, when Solomon dedicated the temple, his last prayer was that God would remember His 'great love' promised to David (2 Chr. 6:42). And through the centuries God had continued to demonstrate that love in a wide variety of different ways.

He had freed His people from slavery and kept them throughout the forty-year journey in the desert because He loved them. Under Joshua, God had enabled them to take back the land, the land He had first promised to their first father Abraham. That too was as an outworking of His love. The same could be said to be true of the constancy of God's care during the times of the Judges, so often contrasted with the fecklessness of the people, and on into the days of Samuel and David. And now, in the days of the Psalm, the travellers had yet another tangible, real and unquestionable demonstration of that love in action, as God rescued them and brought them back to the land first promised to Abraham and then restored in the days of Joshua.

It was only right that the love of God to them reached deep to the very core of their being—to their hearts as well their outer senses.

Love part 2
And if that was true for them, that is surely also true for us today.

We have a much clearer and more profound revelation of God's love.

God planned our rescue from the power and effects of our rebellion—our sin—before time began. And Paul reminds us that this was done 'in love' (Eph. 1:4).

Over and beyond the evidences of that love, found in the Old Testament, God's love stepped into history in the person of the Lord Jesus Christ. Christina Rossetti's poem[5] tells us that 'Love came down at Christmas'—a certainty confirmed in John 3:16.

God's love for us has its roots in eternity and became reality in history—a promise of love that was fleshed out in prophecy but became flesh in a person: the person of God's one and only Son, the Lord Jesus Christ.

Perhaps an even greater wonder is that God's love is personal. Paul reminds us that God demonstrates His love for us in a specific way: that it was while we were still sinners that Christ died for us (Rom. 5:8—look at the use of 'us' and 'we' from v. 1 to v. 8 and then how it continues in v. 9). This demonstration of love is for 'us': an 'us' that includes Paul himself but also all those who, like him, have been justified by faith.

God's plans and purposes are much, much greater than, but are never less than, the words of an old song:

> Wonderful things in the Bible I see:
> This is the dearest, that Jesus loves me....
> Jesus loves even me.[6]

When Peter wrote his second letter, he wrote to those who had a 'faith as precious as ours': and he wrote as one of the apostles of Jesus Christ (2 Peter 1:1–2).

The faith relationship, which each of God's people has with God, has its foundation in God's demonstration of love in Christ's death while we were sinners. It is made real in our lives through a work of regeneration and new birth into a new creation by God Himself, in the person of the Holy Spirit (John 3:7–8; 2 Cor. 5:17).

And God chooses to make His home with us—indeed He chooses to make His home within us (John 14:23; Romans 8:9–11; Col. 1:27).

As a result, we are inseparably bound to the love of God, that is in Christ Jesus our Lord, for all of our lives here on earth (Rom. 8:39).

Response

There is much more that could and should be said about the love of God—a love for each one of His people. It is a love that takes hell-bound sinners and turns them into heaven-bound children of God. It is a love that sets sinners free to serve God in this world and in the place where He takes us.

Whatever else can be said about God's glorious and eternal plans and purposes, there is love. And we are called to respond to that love. This Psalm reminds us that the response is far more than superficial and greater than merely intellectual—it is a love that should touch us and move us to the deepest part of our being.

Film makers know that there are ways of stirring the feelings of the viewers of their films, stirring them to respond with tears. Am I allowed to admit that I am very capable of responding, as expected, to a good weepie? This term, I gather, was first used as a noun about a film nearly one hundred years ago in 1928.[7]

If film makers can cause that response in me, using actors and celluloid, how much more should I respond to the eternal love of God? This love purchased my eternity at the cost of the life of God's Son and now is an indivisible part of my day-by-day living and being.

The responses of the travellers could seem to be at opposite ends of a spectrum of feelings. On the one hand their responses are of joy and laughter. On the other there are weeping and tears. Apart from anything else, these were not the responses of complacency and boredom. They knew, beyond doubt, how marvellous and wonderful were the things God had done for them.

As a 'preachee' (if we can use that word as an opposite of preacher) I find myself more aware of God having dealt with me if I am close to or actually in tears when hearing someone used by God to magnify Jesus, as God's Word is opened. Those tears can be:

- Tears of sorrow—as I am reminded of how my sin required God's son to die for me.

- Tears of wonder—that, knowing all about my past, present and future failings, God's Son should love 'even me'.
- Tears of amazement—that God could allow the same 'even me' to be used in His service (from the same source as the amazement that Paul expresses in 1 Tim. 1:12–17.
- Tears of joy—as I contemplate the prospect of seeing my Saviour on His throne in Heaven or in the skies when He returns as judge of the living and the dead.
- Tears of appreciation—for all that God has done, is doing and promises still to do for all those who are part of His universal family, wherever and whenever they are to be found and, also, in the renewing of God's creation—as God answers the prayer that His will would be done and His Kingdom come, both in part here on earth and fully in the new heavens and the new earth that will one day be revealed.

Have those tears turned to joy and wonder and laughter as I am overwhelmed by love and increasingly know the security and peace that the experience of this love brings? For, as He promised, He will never leave us and is always with us (Heb. 13:5, Matt. 28:20).

For the travellers, as with Paul, that appreciation of God's loving care for them was the motivation for their journey, their way of travelling and what they did when they reached the Land of Promise. We will think a bit more of this in the next chapters of this Book.

Personal reflection

The second half of the 20th century was a period when many programmes and ways of 'doing church' were advocated, including 'Evangelism Explosion', 'Church Down Our Street', 'Purpose Driven' and 'Seeker Friendly' churches with Christians who were contagious. I wonder if there were times when I was tempted to rely on programmes rather than passion.

Passion without the guiding hand of love can become hard and harsh. I need to look back with gratitude to those who, gently but firmly, reminded me of the difference.

Reflection

1. *When was the last time a message from God's Word stirred your heart and soul to the point either of tears or of joy and laughter? Would it be good to thank God and also thank the person who God used in that way, if you have not done so already, of course?*

2. *If you wanted to help someone gain a better appreciation of God's love for them—what parts of the Bible, Christian Books or songs would you point them to? Why? In what specific ways have they helped you? Would that selection have changed over the time you have been one of God's children?*

3. *All of us are different in the way our emotions work. English people are often spoken of as having a 'Stiff*

Upper Lip', which is a way of saying that they are not good with emotions. How do we distinguish between our natural propensity for or against being emotional and a work of God in the person of God the Holy Spirit stirring us up to appreciate and respond to God's love for us?

4. *As you look back to the people God has used to help you, and the ways in which that has happened, how can you be a means that God can use to help others?*

INTRODUCTION TO PART 3

I have had the privilege of knowing people who have the ability to think strategically and put that strategic thinking into practice.

There are also those who are brilliant at getting things done and whose ability to hold in their minds the detail of a whole array of different areas of church life is, to me, quite astonishing.

Yet others would say, of themselves, that they are just pottering along, apparently with neither strategy nor close attention to detail. They are, however, faithful in the things that they do for God and they proclaim the wonderful message of God's good news with honesty and integrity. And God works through them as well.

Then there are the men and women of God it has been my privilege to come to know from different places around the world: people with very different cultural backgrounds and whose church lives and experiences are very different from mine. As a student, I was honoured to know a man who left his wife and family for three years to come to this country to become a better shoemaker. I remember him saying that if he went home at any time in that three-year period, he would never be able to come away again. His love for His Lord shone in his life and was humbling to behold. Then, in more recent years, my wife and I have come to know families who serve God in what we would consider to be very difficult circumstances. Materially they have little by English standards; spiritually they serve God in a country where Christianity is looked down on by many in authority, and health and medical care can easily become an expensive luxury. Yet, in so many ways and with great clarity of purpose, they are truly demonstrating and proclaiming the love of God in Christ to those around them.

In a Book about Adoniram Judson, there is an image of Judson teaching in a Zayat.[1,2] Culturally, pragmatically and in many other ways, this was an appropriate way for Judson to seek to carry out his call to proclaim God's work of salvation in the land now known as Myanmar. Geographically, historically and culturally it is unlikely that this would be as appropriate in another place and time.

So, in this closing section we will look at three principles from this Psalm. The 'How' of how these principles can be applied in our own individual situations will depend on a whole range of circumstances.

This section is being written at a time when the UK Government has recently set out a road map out of a period of lockdown. In the previous twelve months, churches of different sizes have responded to rules and restrictions by using a wide variety of technological and other means to continue serving God. But those responses have, by necessity, been different from the way those churches operated previously.

Has the twelve-month period been a time to reflect on how we will be 'church' in the future? I have heard a number of people say that church will not be the same again or that there will need to be a 'new normal'. But what will that new normal be?

Rend
the heavens

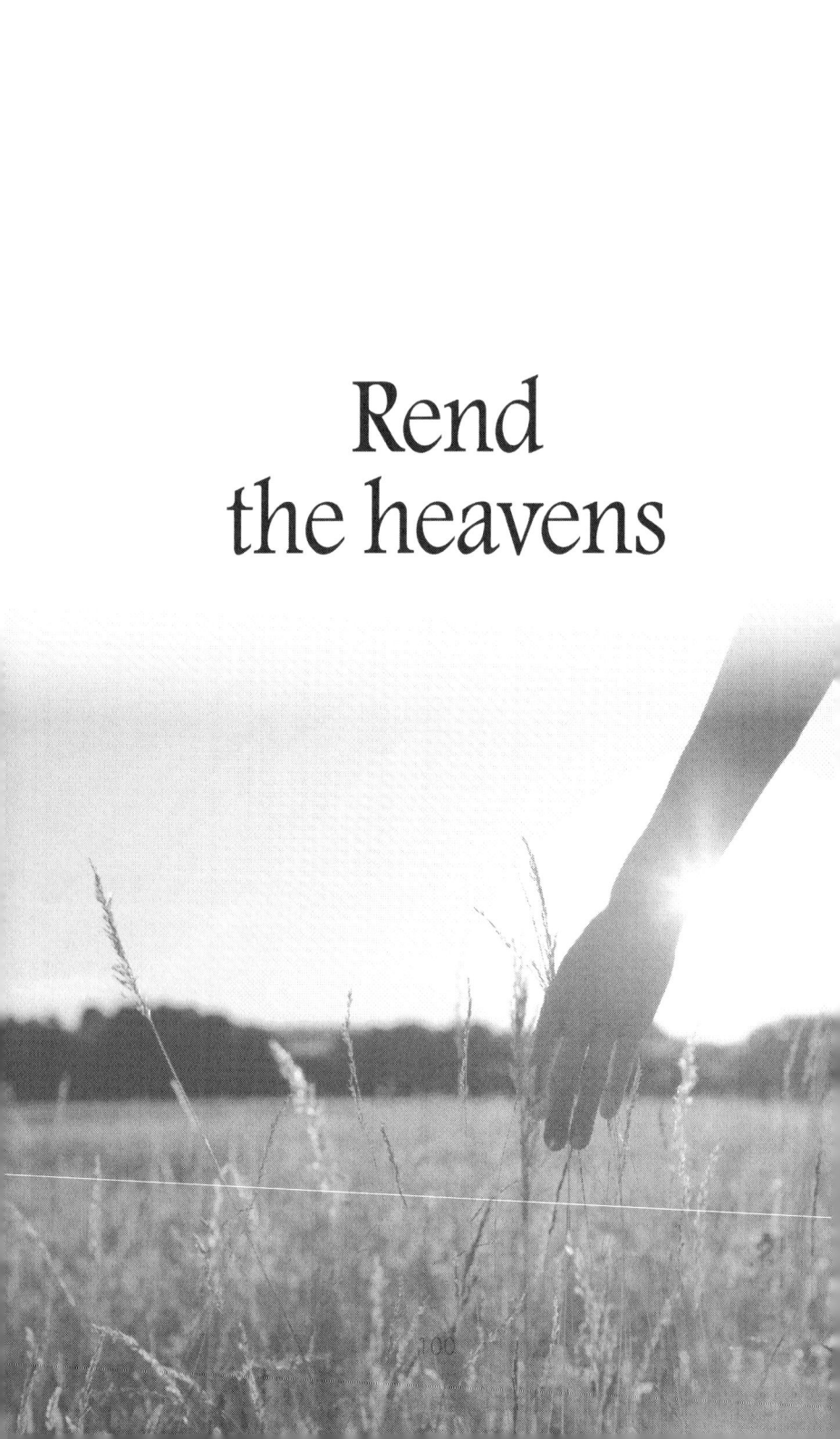

Chapter 8

Who is this Psalm about?

For those who have been brought up in a good Sunday School or in a church which regularly had a children's talk as part of a Sunday morning service, you probably have a fifty per cent chance of giving the right answer without anything else being written.

Was it:

- The Psalmist? Unlike some Psalms, even some of the Songs of Ascents such as Psalms 122, 124, 127, 131 or 133, the Psalmist is not identified.
- The travellers? They are not named or numbered so we are not permitted to know exactly who they were.
- The nations? Again, this is wide ranging and not specific.

In churches which I have attended, when a question was asked in Sunday School or a Sunday morning children's talk, the most likely answers were 'Jesus' or 'God'. And here in this Psalm, it is 'the Lord' on whom the spotlight falls again and again:

- In verse 1, it is the Lord who brought back the captives.
- In verse 2, the nations say that it is the Lord who has done great things.
- In verse 3, the travellers acknowledge that it is indeed the Lord who has done great things for them.

- In verse 4, it is to 'O Lord' that the travellers turn in prayer.

Obvious is it not?

Is it obvious? Surely it must be.

After all, this Psalm is in the book of Psalms which starts with blessings for those who delight in the law of the Lord and ends with a command that everything that has breath should 'praise the Lord' (Ps. 1:2; 150:6). And the book of Psalms is but one of sixty-six books which start with God's creation of the world and finish with God at the heart and centre of His new creation (Gen. 1:1; Rev. 22:1–5).

But, in between these great certainties, there is a hiatus period. It is a hiatus caused by our sins and sinful nature. It is a hiatus that puts us in a state of 'separated-ness' or 'cutoff-ness' from God—for example see Isaiah 59:2.

One image that is sometimes used is based on Deut. 28:23 which talks about a time when the 'sky over your head will be bronze'—impermeable, impenetrable.

All of us who are now on the journey of salvation—the eternal journey of life—spent a period, in effect a lifetime, before we started on that journey. And for all of that period—whether it was long or short—we were cut off from God. We lived in a world that was like a closed box with no access to the universe outside that box.

C. S. Lewis, in a science fiction series, starts with a

description of the earth as 'the Silent Planet' because the earth was cut off from God's heavens.[1]

However, for many of us it is not only our natural state that has caused us to be shut in and shut away from God. For more than 200 years, philosophers, many from Western Europe, have become increasingly confident and strident in the message that if God cannot be proved by some form of human-constructed measuring instrument then He does not or cannot exist. We do not have time to reflect fully on what has happened but a really useful starting point is the work of the late Francis Schaeffer, such as in his books, *Escape from Reason, and Death in the City*.[2] Not only is there a separated-ness as a result of our sin-bent nature and mind set but we are also surrounded by ways of thinking which are assumed to be true—assumptions that leave God to one side as a nonentity or at least an irrelevance.[3]

When we start on the salvation journey, we have to learn to live in the world where God exists and is actively at work. We move from a world in which, for all practical purposes, there is no God to a world where it is in Him that 'we live and move and have our being' (Acts 17:28). It is a 180 degree turn around—from living in a world where God forms zero per cent of our existence to a world where He forms one hundred per cent of everything. Can I suggest that, for many people, this is not an easy transition to make?

Was it different at that time?

The travellers also came from a time when God's people had been cut off from God. They had been separated from God both geographically—in the far-flung corners of the Babylonian Empire—and historically, for seventy years. But there were at least three things they could have kept with them in their time of exile:

- *The law and the prophets*—those parts of the Bible that were written at that time. And, as we have seen in earlier chapters, men like Daniel used the Bible that he had to bring him to God and to plead to God for Him to act in mercy and forgiveness (Dan. 9:18–19).

- *Nattering*—Deut. 6:7 has a specific context in terms of teaching children. It is a command about commandments—a command to talk about them when 'you sit at home and when you walk along the road'. Not a formal time but simply nattering the commands of God as a normal and natural part of everyday life.

- *Personal reminders*—in a Jewish home, even to today, certain mealtimes are reminders of God's dealings with His people, from the weekly *Shabbat* meal to the annual festival of Pesach (Passover). Both would have been possible in a foreign land, even if celebratory songs were too painful to sing in the land of captivity (Ps. 137:4).

The travellers would have been brought up to remember. In turn, as they became adults, they would have become the ones helping others to remember. They would have been a people remembering: remembering God and His covenant dealings with the people of His calling—a virtuous cycle of remembrance which had been or at least should have been part and parcel of the life of God's people from the days of Moses.

The Bible makes it clear that this did not always happen as it should. However, the wording of the Psalm gives evidence that the travellers had remembered and did remember what God had done for them.

Today?

In a book about Revival[4], the author picks up a description of what happened when God was at work in the Western Isles of Scotland between 1949 and 1952.[5] Duncan Campbell, who is identified as someone who was 'involved in' and who 'witnessed' that time of revival, said that what he saw was a 'community saturated with God'. The author, Brian Edwards, picks up that phrase so that the full title of the book is, *Revival! A people saturated with God.*

As that book rightly reminds us, true revival is not something we can manufacture—it is a work of divine grace at a time of God's own choosing.[6] However, are there things we can do to bring people closer to saturation point, including the things mentioned above?

The Bible

Many of us will have seen, in movies or television dramas, a witness in court being asked to promise to tell, 'the truth, the whole truth and nothing but the truth'. If we were to ask Christians if they lived on the basis of 'the Bible, the whole Bible and nothing but the Bible' in determining what they believe and how they should live, I wonder what response we would get?

As Paul says in 2 Timothy 3:15–17 it is the 'Holy Scriptures' which are able to ensure that God's people are 'thoroughly equipped for every good work'. If we have the goal or ambition of being thoroughly equipped, then it is to the Bible, the God-breathed Scriptures, that we must turn.

However, just turning to the Bible, whether by reading it, listening to it read or preached, or indeed by any other means, can provide no certainty that we will become wise for salvation. In a *Desert Island Discs* interview, Aung San Suu Kyi of Myanmar said that she had started reading the Bible at the age of eleven to help her grandfather, whose eyesight was failing. In that interview she said that she loved the language of the Bible but made no mention of it having any other effect on her.[7]

Part of getting a better grip or better understanding of the Bible is to recognize that the Bible speaks to us of:

- *God's Purpose.* God has a purpose that affects the whole of the universe. It is a cosmological purpose to renew this fallen and sin-tarnished creation with a New Heaven and New Earth. For example, see Isa. 65:17 or Rev. 21:1–4. In that New Heaven and New Earth there will be people—God's people—for whom homes are being prepared by their sovereign Saviour. And each and every one of those people will be there because of the fulfilment of God's stated purposes in the Bible—for example in John 20:31: 'these are written that you may believe that Jesus is the Christ ... and that by believing you may have life in his name'.

- *God's Plans.* That purpose did not arrive like a parcel delivered to our doorstep with all the pieces in place. The Bible contains a progressive revealing of that purpose in plans and promises from the start of Genesis through all the various parts of both the Old and New Testaments in the Bible.[8] Some parts of those plans and promises are readily easy to see, such as those read or referred to during services in the Christmas period. Others can take more work to pick out and identify.

- *A Person.* But one thing is utterly clear—not least because Jesus tells us so Himself: the Bible is about a person. That person is God and especially in the person of God's eternal Son, the Lord Jesus Christ. This is most clearly stated in the accounts of Jesus' meetings following His resurrection in Luke's gospel (Luke 24:25–27; 44–46).

In Luke 24:45, it was Christ that opened the minds of the disciples. These were people who had spent three years walking and talking with Him, eating and drinking with Him, listening to His teaching and being witnesses of His miraculous power. Yet still they could not understand without Him opening their minds. John, just a page or so later, humbly admits that it was not until after Jesus' resurrection that they believed: both the Bible and the words that Jesus said (John 2:22). True understanding of the Bible only comes as God is at work in a person's mind and heart!

How good are we at preparing the soil for God's work by helping people to see and understand the great themes of the Bible—to see that it is much more than a book with lovely language?

Nattering

In the New Testament, the early Christians were driven out of Jerusalem and wherever the scattered church went, the people 'preached' the Word (Acts 8:4). The believers were Jews or, in some cases, those who had become Jews from non-Jewish backgrounds. They were people who had been taught to talk when 'you sit at home and when you walk along the road' (Deut. 6:7). Many have suggested that the word, 'preach', in this verse could better be understood as gossiping the gospel or perhaps nattering the news.

When we get together with our friends and neighbours— when we are waiting in line in a shop or sitting near someone on a bus or train—what do we natter, chatter or gossip about? In the UK, we have a reputation for having an obsession with the weather. Then for some it would be to do with sport and, for many months during the period of Covid lockdowns, everyone developed a passion for statistics (whether it be the number of reported cases or the number of people who had received a vaccination).

Where does nattering the news of Jesus Christ fit in?

Are we helped, trained or encouraged in our churches to develop the ability to talk about our Saviour and His wonderful love for us—personally, individually and in a way that draws people to want to find out more? And not just those who are 'full time' or 'part time' Christian workers.

I used to get upset when people sent me questionnaires about 'hobbies' and in the list of hobbies being a Christian was of no greater importance than angling or model railways. To my shame, I wonder if I could speak as easily about eternal life as I could about stamp collecting—a childhood hobby.

Looking back, nattering was probably easier to do when

I was a church minister. People expected me to do so—
even if some might discount much of what I said because
it was my job to say things about God and Jesus. The
people of Acts 8:4 were those, other than the apostles,
who remained in Jerusalem—Acts 8:1. It was the non-
apostles who nattered about their God and Saviour, and so
the news spread.

Hospitality/relationships

From time to time, a good friend (from a Jewish background
who had come to know the promised Christ as His Saviour)
used to come to our church and lead a Passover meal.
It gave us the chance to invite friends, neighbours and
teachers from local schools to come and share a meal with
us. These teachers were interested because the Jewish
festivals were part of the Religious Education lessons that
they taught. The Passover was faithful in its content but,
at the same time, our friend pointed again and again to the
one whose life, death and resurrection perfectly fulfilled
the hopes and longings expressed in the *Haggadah*—the
order of the Passover meal.

There are many ways in which special events can allow
us to build or develop relationships with people, which in
turn can be used to bring people closer to seeing God in all
His saving glory—seeing Him in the lives and actions as
well as the words of God's people. Both the Alpha Course
and Christianity Explored use informal times around food

to allow relationships to develop among those who are attending.

How can we make better use of special times of the year or special events? Can we use events which are directly Christian as well as others which are not? How do we do so in formal church settings and in our homes to provide a locale where God can make Himself known?

Personal reflection

As a family, we are privileged to be part of a church that has a number of people skilled in preaching and teaching God's Word. They are different in who they are and how they preach and teach. Why is it that some preachers encourage me more than others? Perhaps the same could be said of choices we make about Christian conferences or holidays— does the name of a speaker or the musicians or even the organization running such an event make me more likely to book than if there were other names linked to what was happening? This is not necessarily wrong. If they have been used by God to help people know and appreciate more of His Son our Saviour—that is a good thing to desire. (If it is a matter of eloquence or musical tastes that reflect our own or the quality of the jokes—that is another thing.)

When I hear or sing the following hymn, do I mean it as much as I want to mean it?

> More about Jesus would I know,
> More of His grace to others show;

More of His saving fulness see,

More of His love who died for me. ...

More, more about Jesus ...[9]

Reflections

1. On a cold frosty morning, I have to spend time defrosting my car windscreen to be able to see what is in front of me. Are there things in my life or my church that can obscure the view of God—things that could and should be cleaned away?

2. What books and other means would you recommend to others to help them have God front and centre in their lives? Are there things that you yourself could read again, or in some other way remind yourself, to encourage your focus on Him?

3. In what ways has the Lord done great things for you? How do you reveal your response to those great things?

Blessing

For forty years, Moses led God's people from slavery in Egypt to freedom in the Land of Promise. During those forty years, the people encountered a wide variety of problems including hunger and drought, punishment for disobedience and doubt, and also dealing with the many nations that lived in the land through which they travelled.

On two occasions, when travelling through the land occupied by the Edomites—descendants of Esau—and the Amorites, Moses attempted to use diplomacy as a means of easing their journey through those two countries. In both cases, Moses asked for permission to pass through the land, using and not abusing the 'King's Highway'. Sadly, diplomacy failed and in both cases the request was refused. The requests are found in Numbers 20:17; 21:22. For example:

> Please let us pass through your country. We will not go through any field or vineyard, or drink water from any well. We will travel along the King's Highway and not turn to the right or to the left until we have passed through your territory.

The English 'Countryside Code' tells us to 'Respect, Protect and Enjoy' the places that we visit in England and Wales.[1]

Moving away from travel and enjoying the countryside, the oath attributed to Hippocrates—an oath to do with medical practice—is often said to start with the words, 'First, do no harm.'[2]

There have been times in my Christian life when, to my shame, I have not even reached that fairly basic standard of thinking, speaking or doing. However, from Abraham onwards, God's promise to and through His people has been not that we would be harmless but a blessing. So, for example in Genesis 12:2–3, God says to Abraham:

> I will bless you ...
>
> you will be a blessing.
>
> I will bless those who bless you ...
>
> all peoples on earth will be blessed through you.

At this point we really should spend time tracing through both Old and New Testaments to see how that idea of receiving blessing and transmitting blessing are developed in God's Word. However, time and space do not allow for that, so let us take just two examples from Proverbs 11 (ESV):

> By the blessing of the upright a city is exalted (v. 11),
>
> Whoever brings blessing will be enriched (v. 25).

And, in the New Testament, Peter says:

> Do not repay evil for evil or reviling for reviling, but on the contrary, bless, for to this you were called, that you may obtain a blessing (1 Peter 3:9).

But how can we put this into practice?

Collateral blessing

When someone becomes one of God's people—when they set off with Christ on the journey that will eventually lead them to heaven—there are changes that take place in who they are and how they live.

At one level it is a total transformation of who they are. Jesus talked about a new birth (John 3:3), Paul spoke of a new creation (2 Cor. 5:17) and used the image of someone having died and been buried and then being raised from death to live a new life (Rom. 6:3–4).

But, alongside that transformation, is the developing and growing change that takes place in our lives as God works in us, in the person of God the Holy Spirit. For example, He is the one who sanctifies us (Rom. 15:16) and who produces fruit in our lives (Gal. 5:22–24). Knowing that He is at work in us, we are to keep in step with the Spirit (Gal. 5:5) and grow up into Christ (Eph. 4:14–16).

As God does make those changes in our lives, they will have—they must surely have—a real world impact in a whole variety of ways.

- Is your workplace or neighbourhood a more tranquil environment, even in the middle of turmoil, because your life demonstrates the peace of God that passes understanding (Phil. 4:7)? I can look back to times when that peace has been very tangible in difficult situations—and other times when I have 'lost it'.

- What about your neighbours? Are their doors open or shut to you and are your doors open or shut to them?

- Are you trusted by colleagues and those that you work for?
- How good are you at keeping secrets? Both as a former lawyer and church minister, I was entrusted with information that I had to keep to myself. The ability to be trusted with secrets should be true of all God's people and not just those who are lawyers or ministers.

There is an old poem which says:

> For me 'twas not the truth you taught
> To you so clear, to me still dim
> But when you came to me you brought
> A sense of Him.

> And from your eyes He beckons me,
> And from your heart His love is shed,
> Til I lose sight of you and see
> The Christ instead.[3]

Part of that change in our lives and living flows from the fact that we stand daily and hourly in the sight of God who knows the secrets of our hearts, not least because He has chosen to make His home with us and in us (John 14:23; Rom. 8:9–11).

Considered blessing

However, there could and should be blessing that comes from consideration and planning—God's people considering and deciding how they live in ways which bring God's blessing on all the nations. As we saw earlier, it was a consideration of the Lord's Prayer that formed the foundation of William Carey's 'Inquiry'. His desire to see God's will done on earth encompassed many aspects of life. In their book, *Carey, Christ and Cultural Transformation*[4], Ruth and Vishal Mangalwadi ask, 'Who was William Carey?' and then suggest a number of possible answers including the following:

- Botanist—one species of Eucalyptus found only in India is named after him.
- Engineer—he introduced the steam engine to India and encouraged locals to copy his design using local materials and skills.
- Economist—he introduced the idea of Savings Banks.
- Medicine—he led a campaign for the humane treatment of leprosy patients.
- Agriculture—he founded an Agri-Horticultural Society some thirty years before the Royal Horticultural Society was founded in England.
- Literature—he translated and published Indian religious classics and works of philosophy and gave value to local languages such as Bengali.
- Education—this man who had started as a village cobbler became Professor of Bengali, Sanskrit and Marathi.
- Libraries—he set up a system of lending libraries.

- Forestry—he put into practice humanity's responsibility for the earth and thought that 'the wilderness will, in every respect, become a fruitful field'.[5]
- Social science—in particular standing against the oppression of women.

There are many more items in the list including Public Administration, linking Ethics to Religion, Printing and Newspaper Publishing, Mathematics and Astronomy, and the study of History. But overall, Carey 'was an evangelist who used every available medium to illumine every dark facet of ... life with the light of truth'.[6]

Not many of us have the ability or opportunity to be involved in quite so many areas of life as William Carey! However, there are many examples of God's people, with a dedication and focus in one area, bringing blessing to people in different places around the world.

For example, in the book, *Under the Thorn Tree*, Richard Bewes reports that an Irish medical researcher and medical specialist, talking about leprosy settlements he had visited in many places around the world, said that wherever he went those running them would 'invariably be Christians'.[7]

Closer to home, Richard Bewes also refers to Anthony Ashley-Cooper, the 7th Earl of Shaftesbury—known as the 'Poor Man's Earl'[8]. He became God's instrument, among other things, both to end some of the iniquities of children's employment in factories, coal mines and as chimney sweeps and also to provide education through the Ragged Schools Union.

In Ezra 1:4, it is the planning of the Persian Emperor which provided the tangible blessing of silver, gold, goods and livestock to the people who accepted the invitation to journey back to God's Land of Promise. And that provision was seen and acknowledged by the nations.

How do we plan or consider planning blessing that can flow from the blessings we receive as God's people?

Part of the reasons for quoting that long list about William Carey is a reminder to me, should I need one, that I am not him. Such skills, gifts and abilities as most of us have are much more limited. But, in God's goodness, we each have skills, gifts and abilities that can be used by God for His glory and for the blessing of others.

If that is true of an individual, it is also true of a group of God's people—a church. The gifting which God has given to any one church will be different from that of others. It does not have to mean less or fewer: it is simply different. But what it does mean is that we need to be wise in assessing what it is that any one group of God's people attempt to do. However, let us never forget something that William Carey himself said:

> Expect great things from God; attempt great things for God.[9]

Alongside that, is the recognition that individual

areas, individual communities, are made up of different groups of people and have different sets of needs. One thing which took me time to learn to do, when working in an area near Southampton, was to get to know and seek help from Local Government staff in the area. Whatever their religious affiliations, they had knowledge and information which was not immediately available to me as the minister of a church. So, when I was then asked to help another church in a different area, one of the first meetings I arranged was with staff from the local town council. They gave me an insight into the town, which I had not gained from anyone else.

There have been programmes on television which ask one of two people, who think they know each other well, questions about the other one. The idea is to see whether both give the same answer to the same question.

If you were asked to name, say, five significant needs in your own locality, based on what those living in that locality felt were important, what would your answer be? Would your answers be the same as those of a random group of people from the streets around your church? At one time our church did use a questionnaire about the local community when visiting homes in the nearby area.

Men like Anthony Ashley-Cooper saw clear and obvious needs and applied their Christian faith to alleviating those needs. That ability to assess needs and to seek to be a blessing has continued through the years and is still seen in many ways today. For example, Basics Banks and Food Banks, Christians Against Poverty, Street Pastors and many more.

However, work that may be appropriate in a university town may not be needed in a retirement area on the coast and rural communities as well as more urban settings need to know the reality of God's love in the Lord Jesus Christ in ways that are relevant to their situation.

How strategic is our thinking and planning? How do we change strategic thinking into action—using the most precious resource God has given to the church: that of His children?

Community blessing

When God's Kingdom comes, when His will is done on earth, there is blessing for His people. But the scope and sweep of that blessing extends beyond the church into the wider community. The book, *Revival: a people saturated with God*, took the second part of its title from Duncan Campbell's comments on God's work in the Western Isles of Scotland. However, the actual quotation talked of a 'community saturated with God'.[10] Later on the same page, there is a longer comment from Duncan Campbell which, in part, describes revival as 'a going of God among His people, and an awareness of God laying hold of the community'.

As mentioned in Chapter 2, the Authorised King James Version translation of Acts 17:6 talks of Christians as people who had 'turned the world upside down'. Other translations talk about people who have 'caused trouble all over the world'. Perhaps that is not surprising from the mouths of those who have much to lose when Jesus Christ truly takes hold of people and of communities. In Philippi, slave owners lost a lucrative income from a demon-possessed girl (Acts 16:16–19). In Ephesus, the makers of idols saw their money-making skills losing their appeal to those who would no longer visit the great Temple in the heart of the city (Acts 19:24–27).

There are many examples over the centuries of great changes when there is truly an 'awareness of God laying hold of the community'.

A former Archbishop of Canterbury once said that 'The Church exists primarily for the sake of those who are still outside it.'[11]

When we are making plans, whether that is personally or as part of a body of God's people, what share of our planning has to do with what happens outside the walls of our church building and what share is to do with those who are already on the inside? Both are necessary, both indeed.

Our current church uses the model of a circle or cycle for church life.[12]

SERVE

to   to

RELEASE   REACH

to   to

GROW

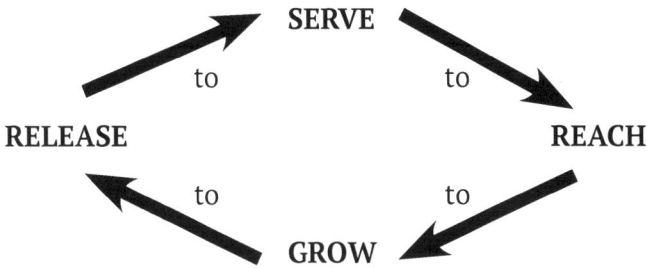

The aim is to apply that cycle to every part of the church's life. It starts with the imperative of service.

Crucial blessing

That image also reminds us that there is an ultimate blessing—a blessing that should always be in our minds and thinking.

While service in and of itself is a good thing—a blessing to those who are served—there is a greater blessing for which we should long for those who are being served.

Over a lockdown period in the UK, my wife and I had the opportunity, on behalf of our church, to take small gifts of food treats and wonderfully prepared flowers to some isolated elderly people in two sheltered-housing blocks.

As we have come to know the people as people, not just names on a list, we are thinking about how we can take things forward—not just into church but more importantly into God's Kingdom for all eternity.

Personal reflections

In my student days, I remember someone once saying that the church speaks of 'out reach' but it practices 'in grab'.[13] During my time in church leadership, it was easy to judge myself, and feel that others were judging me, by what happened inside the church's building and especially in the times when the church met together on the Lord's day. Are the images used by the Lord Jesus Christ of salt and light more helpful than just thinking about seats occupied on a Sunday morning?

It has been a genuine pleasure to be able to be part of blessing being given to people in our local community. Small gifts, generously given for the church to use, have been received with gratitude. If it had not been for the difficult times brought about by the pandemic, would those opportunities have existed?

Reflection

1. *Where are the places that God will take you in the next five days? Can you suggest two or perhaps three areas of need in each of those places? How are you placed to have an impact of blessing on those places?*

2. *Looking at the body of God's people in which God has placed you—what blessings have come from His hands in the last six months? Jacob wrestled with God on the basis that he would not let God go until God blessed him (Gen. 32:26). Do your wrestling skills need developing?*

3. *What means do you use to assess the needs of your specific local community? Is there any danger in hearing about a 'solution' (at a Christian conference for example) and then trying to find a problem to fix with it?*

4. *What changes would there be if God's Kingdom came and God's will was done in the streets around your church?*

Will

I would suspect that at least once a year—and perhaps more often than that—we will read or hear read or even hear someone preaching about the visit of the 'Wise Men' to Bethlehem via Jerusalem.

It is a passage that has particular memories for me as one of our local schools used to do a short series in their Religious Education lessons on the 'Wise men and their Gifts'. Over a few years this developed into the following:

- • Session 1—children with their teachers discussing and noting down what they 'knew' about the story.
- • Session 2—taking them back to Matthew Chapter 2 to see that what they 'knew' was not actually in the Bible at all.
- • Session 3—looking at the actual story to consider the significance of the three gifts and, ideally, to recognize that the wise men came with one purpose—to worship God's Son, our Saviour.

When looking at the story, we can focus on the Wise Men (Magi), the nature and purpose of their gifts, the town they were directed to visit, Herod and his attempted deception or the way in which God kept Joseph and his family safe. I cannot recall hearing anyone speak on a simple word found in Matthew 2:6. It is the word 'will': 'out of you "will" come a ruler....' And He did!

It is that same word which forms the bedrock of confidence at the end of Psalm 126. It is there in v. 5—'will reap'—and also in v. 6—'will return'.

That certainty flows from:
- What God has done (vv. 1–3).
- Their prayer to God (v. 4).

In 1872, a fictional story was published about a twelve-year-old American girl under the title, *What Katy Did*. Some sequels followed, one of which was *What Katy Did Next*.[1]

In essence, what the travellers were doing is looking at 'What God did (had done)', and then, on the basis of what they then knew to be true about God, looked forward to 'What God would do next'.

In looking through the book of Isaiah over a period of weeks (as a series in our church), the word, 'will', started catching my attention with increasing regularity. It was a word that had been drawn to my attention when as a young Christian, I was first taken to do some door-to-door visiting. Those who were leading the time, prayed from Isa. 55:11—that, as promised, God's Word 'will not return to [Him] empty'. There are a large number of 'will' promises from God about His Word in that chapter alone.

Then, you could look at Isa. 58:11–12 concerning God who 'will' guide, satisfy needs and strengthen and, as a result, there will be blessings of a well-watered garden, rebuilt ruins and other linked images. There are further 'will' promises in Isaiah 60: 1–7, 13–14, and Isaiah 61 which speaks of the one sent to proclaim what will happen in vv. 3–7.

A godly friend used to remind me of what Paul says in Eph. 3:20: 'Chris: don't forget that God can do more than all we ask and imagine.' Absolutely, certainly, gloriously, wonderfully—yes of course He can.

However, I wonder if in my own heart God's 'can' speaks to potential and possibility, but God's 'will' takes me further—that leads me to anticipation and expectancy. If God has said that something 'will' happen then surely that should have me sitting on the edge of my seat just waiting for the 'when' of that happening (way beyond asking 'if' it might happen).

For example, when thinking about the Parable of the Sower, the same seed but four different types of soil (Luke 8:4–15), do I focus on the 'if' of wondering which type of soil a particular person's heart might be—or on the fact that, in most farmers' fields, the great majority of the soil and the greater part of the field is good? Is the question how fruitful will the harvest be, not whether there will be a harvest at all? So, in John 4:35, Jesus calls on his followers to pray for workers for the harvest for 'the fields … are ripe for harvest'.

Two questions:

HOW DO WE KNOW WHAT IS GOD'S 'WILL'?

There are some things that do not apply to us today in exactly the same way as they did to the people of Israel before the incarnation, crucifixion and resurrection of the Lord Jesus Christ. One obvious example is that the travellers in this Psalm were travelling back to a promised home in a Jerusalem under the continuing power of a

Persian Emperor. In the centuries since this Psalm was written, that land has known occupation and rule by many of the different superpowers of their day. And, more importantly, the home now promised to God's people is the one to be found in 'my Father's house' (John 14:2). Perhaps one answer to that question can be found in Psalm 37:4–5. There we are told:

> Delight yourself in the LORD,
>
> and He will give you the desires of your heart.
>
> Commit your way to the LORD;
>
> trust in him, and He will do this.

WHAT ARE WE TO DO?

Brian Edwards quotes the late Dr Martin Lloyd-Jones who said that 'The Church is not meant always to be in a state of revival but is always to do ordinary everyday work.'[2] And that certainly seems to be true of the travellers when they returned to the Land. The things that they are recorded as doing are ordinary and everyday—they go out sowing seed, carrying seed to sow. The thing that marks them out, however, is their tears, their weeping. For, in the same place, Brian Edwards continues with the quotation that sometimes we can get so used to the ordinary and everyday that we 'forget that the church is meant to have special occasions'. When I was growing up, an Irish comedian, Jimmy Cricket, used as a catch phrase, 'Come 'ere! There's more.'[3]

That is the certainty that saw the travellers undertake the ordinary and everyday—that God's 'will' gave them a reason to hope for more—more than sowing and more than weeping but an expectation of reaping and joy.

There is much to be said but at this point I want to go and seek God—to seek Him for family, friends, neighbourhood and church. I want to learn to wrestle more but to do so in the expectation that God will bring to pass His good, pleasing and perfect will (Rom. 12:2). There is a companion book to *Revival! A people saturated with God* which is simply called, *Praying for Revival.*[4]

May we see more and more of God's people going about their daily business and their ordinary, everyday work in the church with tears in their eyes—tears that flow because they are pleading with God to give us cause for songs of joy: joy among the young people who have their lives ahead of them; joy for those who are close to the end of their journey; joy in each and every part of life; joy because God's 'will' is seen and known and we see His Kingdom come in the community and country in which each one of us lives.

Personal reflection

It used to be said that we should employ teenagers while they still know everything. At the risk of betraying my age even more clearly, has my expectation and anticipation—my eagerness and longing for God to be at work—become swallowed up in the ordinary and the everyday over the last years or decades?

Having retired from work a few months ago, there has been time to start on clearing out my study. Part of that has been seeing if long-neglected books are worth reading again. Many of them have proved to be a real encouragement as I have been reminded of things that helped me in my walk with God many years ago—and can still help me now.

Reflections

1. How do you encourage your heart to be expectant—to be certain that God is a God of 'will'?

2. What is God's good, pleasing and perfect will for each one of us in the places God has called us to serve Him? Do we work, pray, plead and serve on the basis that it is a 'when' and not an 'if' that there will be times of songs of joy. Jesus, in Luke 15, spoke of rejoicing in heaven over the repentance of one sinner. There must be a rolling thunder of rejoicing as the multitude without number from around the world (from Rev. 7:8) are, one by one, welcomed into God's family. Who will be among this number that you are serving and seeking to bless?

3. Can you find others that will share a longing for God to bring about His 'will'? In Psalm 126:5 it is 'those' plural who are to sow in tears.

REFERENCES

Bewes, Richard, *Under the Thorn Tree*, (Fearn, Ross-shire: Christian Focus, 2017).

Bonar, Horatius, *The Word of Promise*, (Ambassador Productions, 1986).

Bunyan, John, *The Pilgrim's Progress*, Children's Illustrated Classics Edition, (London: J. M. Dent, 1964).

Edwards, Brian H., *Revival! A people saturated with God*, (Welwyn Garden City: Evangelical Press, first published in 1990 and now available through Day One Publications).

Edwards, Brian H., *Praying for Revival*, (Leominster: Day One Publications, 2019).

Hulse, Erroll, *Adoniram Judson and the Missionary Call*, (Leeds: Reformation Today Trust, 1966).

Lewis, C. S., *The Horse and his Boy*, (London: Grafton, 2002).

Lewis, C. S., *The Screwtape Letters*, (London: Fontana, 1971 Impression).

Mangalwadi, Ruth and Vishal, *Carey, Christ and Cultural Transformation*, (Noida, India: OM Publishing, 1993).

M'Cheyne, Robert Murray, *The Works of the Late Rev. Robert Murray M'Cheyne*, (New York: Robert Carter, 1847). https://www.grace-ebooks.com/library

Ryle, J. C., *Holiness*, (Louisville, KY: Evangelical Press, 2014).

Schaeffer, Francis, *Death in the City*, (Westmont, Illinois: IVP, first UK Edition in 1969).

Schaeffer, Francis, *Escape from Reason*, (Westmont, Illinois: IVP, 1968).

Spurgeon, C. H., *The Treasury of David—3 Volumes*, (McLean, Virginia: Macdonald Publishing Co., 1975).

ENDNOTES

Introduction

1 Taken from: https://www.kiplingsociety.co.uk/poem/poems_serving. htm.

Chapter 1

1 Spurgeon, C. H., *The Treasury of David – 3 volumes*, (McLean, Virginia: Macdonald Publishing Co., 1975), p.68.

2 Naftali Silberberg, a Jewish scholar, quoted online, says:

Many interpretations have been given for these ambiguous words. Here are a few of them:

a) In the Holy Temple courtyard, there was an ultra-wide stairway that consisted of fifteen large, semi-circular steps that 'ascended' into the inner section of the courtyard. The Levites, whose job it was to accompany the Temple service with song and instrumental music, would stand on these steps and sing these fifteen psalms.

b) These psalms were sung on a high 'ascendant' musical note.

c) These psalms were sung starting in a low tone of voice and steadily ascending to a higher one.

d) These psalms were sung by the Jews who ascended from Babylon to Israel in the time of Ezra the Scribe.

e) These psalms were sung by the Jews when they would 'ascend' to visit the Holy Temple three times annually for the festivals.

f) These psalms praise, exult and 'elevate' God.

There is yet another interpretation given about David building the foundations for the temple but, as the building of the Temple was carried out by Solomon after David's death, it has not been included. https://www.chabad.org/library/article_cdo/ aid/655450/jewish/What-is-a-Song-of-Ascents.htmm

3 Ancient Iran | British Museum https://www.britishmuseum.org/ collection/galleries/ancient-iran

4 https://www.britannica.com/biography/Herodotus-Greek-historian

5 The distance is almost certainly a case of 'not bothering to spoil

a good story with facts'. For, we are told that, when the Marathon was first run as part of the Olympics in the modern era it was not the same length as it is today. The current length arose as a result of the route used in the 1908 Olympic Games in London which needed to finish outside Buckingham Palace. https://www.history.com/news/why-is-a-marathon-26-2-miles

6   https://idioms.thefreedictionary.com/the+gospel+truth.

Chapter 2

1   I believe that work started on the Cathedral in 1220 and the spire itself was finished about 100 years later. The spire only became the tallest when the spire at Lincoln Cathedral collapsed. See, for example, https://www.salisburycathedral.org.uk/history/adding-spire / https://en.wikipedia.org/wiki/Salisbury_Cathedral.

2   Evidently the film makers used a measure of artistic licence and the wonderful view shown in the film is some fifteen miles from the Golden Valley itself: https://www.movie-locations.com/movies/s/Shadowlands.php

3   Many will recognise Isa. 61:1–2 which was read by Jesus Christ (see Luke 4:18–19).

4   'God Always Keeps His Promises' by Kauflin, Bob, and Althoff, Jon, (Sovereign Grace Music) https://sovereigngracemusic.org/music/songs/god-always-keeps-his-promises/

5   In England all Local Authority maintained schools are required by law to hold a daily act of 'Collective Worship' (sometimes called 'Assemblies'). These gatherings are to be 'wholly or mainly of a broadly Christian character'— for example see Schedule 20 in the School Standards and Framework Act 1998 (legislation.gov.uk)

6   Ryle, J. C., *Holiness*, (Grand Rapids, MI: Evangelical Press, undated). The copy I have was priced at 50p— probably the best 50p I have ever spent!

7   Taken from David Livingstone Quotes (Author of Missionary Travels and Researches in South Africa) (goodreads.com). https://www.goodreads.com/author/quotes/211925.David_Livingstone

8 Refrain added to the hymn, 'Come we that love the Lord' by Isaac Watts (1674–1748).

9 From the hymn, 'Abide with me', by H. F. Lyte (1793–1847).

10 From the hymn, 'I saw a new vision of Jesus', by W. V. Higham, (1926–2016).

11 From the hymn, 'There is a higher throne' by Keith and Kristyn Getty, https://www.music-ministry.org/hymns/there-is-a-higher-throne/

12 'Standing on the promises of Christ my King', by Russell Kelso Carter (1849–1928). https://www.hymnal.net/en/hymn/h/340

Chapter 3

1 For example: https://www.thegospelcoalition.org/blogs/justin-taylor/the-pattern-of-the-kingdom-gods-people-in-gods-place-under-gods-rule/

2 Taken from https://christianhistoryinstitute.org/study/module/carey A really fascinating view of the work of God through William Carey (written by a Christian couple in India) is: Mangalwadi, Ruth and Vishal, *Carey, Christ and Cultural Transformation*, (Noida: OM Publishing, 1993).

3 This extract copied from Holiness (apuritansmind.com). http://www.apuritansmind.com/wp-content/uploads/FREEEBOOKS/Holiness-J.C.Ryle.pdf

4 Latimer and Ridley Burned at the Stake | History Today. https://www.historytoday.com/archive/months-past/latimer-and-ridley-burned-stake

5 From the hymn, 'A Debtor to Mercy Alone' (Augustus M. Toplady, 1740–1778).

6 Ryle, J. C., *Holiness*, (Grand Rapids, Michigan: Evangelical Press, undated), p. 72.

7 Bunyan, John, *The Pilgrim's Progress*, Children's Illustrated Classics Edition, (London: J. M. Dent, 1964), pp. 109–110.

8 Ibid., p. 13.

9 From the hymn, 'Come Thou fount of every blessing' by Robert Robinson (1735–1790).

Chapter 4

1   Janet Street Preacher, Dec 2018. https://lewes.co.uk/forum/post/ Wycherley_twaddle/258613

2   https://www.britannica.com/place/Negev

3   In the Authorised King James Version, there is an echo in this verse to Psalm 126:1 — God was going to 'bring again the captivity' of Jacob's tents.

4   I have heard it said that God has (at least) five answers to our prayers:

1. Yes

2. No

3. Wait [If you are anything like me — not an easy answer to deal with]

4. Mind your own business [C. S. Lewis uses the phrase, 'No one is told any story but their own', in some of his books, for example, *The Horse and his Boy*, (London: Grafton, 2002), p. 158]

5. Do it yourself.

All are possible answers from God, all equally valid and given according to His good, pleasing and perfect will (Rom. 12:2).

5   The hymn, 'There shall be showers of blessing' by D. W. Whittle (1840 – 1901).

Introduction to Part 2

1   From the hymn, 'We limit not the truth of God', (George Rawson, 1807 – 1889).

2   Found at: https://www.azquotes.com/author/13978-Charles_ Spurgeon/tag/eternity.

Chapter 5

1   This is the third time so far that journeys and especially summer holiday journeys have sprung to mind. This book was written after almost a year of intermittent lockdowns during the Covid pandemic. As I write, the thought of having the freedom to travel,

whether within the UK or elsewhere, seems like a dream. How much more it must have been for God's people after seventy years of lockdown!

2   'The Fallen Caryatid Carrying her Stone', Auguste Rodin, c.1880–1, cast 1950 | Tate. https://www.tate.org.uk/art/artworks/rodin-the-fallen-caryatid-carrying-her-stone-n05955

3   From https://www.goodreads.com/author/quotes/205.Robert_A_Heinlein

4   It was suggested that I gave up art at an early stage in my school life—probably as a benefit to the world of art!

5   From the hymn, 'Standing on the promises of Christ my King', by Russell Kelso Carter (1849–1928). https://www.hymnal.net/en/hymn/h/340

6   For some 300 pages of closely printed promises see Horatius Bonar's book, *The Word of Promise*, (Ambassador Productions, 1986). Even this book the author confirms is a selection not a collection of God's promises. https://www.amazon.co.uk/Word-Promise-Handbook-Promises-Scripture-ebook/dp/B07NPWQH9L

7   Daredevils of Niagara Falls | The Tightrope Walkers (imaxniagara.com)

8   From the hymn, 'There's a way back to God' by E. H. Swinstead, (1882–1950). https://www.praise.org.uk/hymn/theres-a-way-back-to-god/

Chapter 6

1   http://teddiesfortragedies.org.uk/

2   Probably originally by Charles Spurgeon but put slightly differently: https://www.goodreads.com/quotes/327237-the-day-we-find-the-perfect-church-it-becomes-imperfect
   In this version, for example, from Billy Graham: https://www.azquotes.com/quote/697892

3   Lewis, C. S., *The Screwtape Letters*, (London: Fontana, 1971 Impression), p. 15.

Chapter 7

1 I think they were mostly reprints of single sermons and, again, mostly of preachers from the 1800s.

2 M'Cheyne, Robert Murray, 'The Love of Christ'—quotations taken from an online pdf copy of *The Works of The Late Rev. Robert Murray M'Cheyne*—Sermon XXX, (New York: Robert Carter, 1847): https://www.grace-ebooks.com/library/Robert%20Murray%20MCheyne/RMM_The%20Works%20of%20the%20Late%20Rev%20Robert%20Murray%20MCheyne%20Vol%202.pdf

3 Or controls us (ESV or NASB) or constraineth us (AKJV) and it is this last word that was the one M'Cheyne responded to. Towards the end of his message, M'Cheyne talks about God having 'invented a way of *drawing us ...*' M'Cheyne, Robert Murray, 'The Love of Christ', Sermon XXX, p. l0.

4 M'Cheyne. Robert Murray, 'The Love of Christ', p. 2.

5 Rossetti, Christina, 'Love Came Down at Christmas, 1885 – better known as a Christmas Carol. https://en.wikipedia.org/wiki/Love_Came_Down_at_Christmas

6 From the hymn, 'I am so glad that our Father in Heaven' by Philip Paul Bliss (1838–1876): https://www.hymnal.net/en/hymn/h/291.

7 https://www.etymonline.com/word/weepy.
One film of 1928 was described as a 'startlingly ambitious, epic weepie-romance' in a 2018 review. ://www.theguardian.com/film/2018/feb/01/shiraz-a-romance-of-india-review

Introduction to Part 3

1 Hulse, Erroll, *Adoniram Judson and the Missionary Call*, (Leeds: Reformation Today Trust, 1966), p. 37.

2 https://en.wikipedia.org/wiki/Zayat

Chapter 8

1 https://www.britannica.com/topic/Out-of-the-Silent-Planet

2 Schaeffer, Francis, *Escape from Reason* (Westmont, Illinois: IVP,

1968); Schaeffer, Francis, *Death in the City* (Westmont, Illinois: IVP, first UK Edition in 1969).

3   I do appreciate that what is said in this paragraph may not apply equally to all countries and cultures around the world. Schaeffer was an American who had grown up before World War II and many of the people he and his wife cared for came from either Western Europe, including the UK, or his home country.

4   Edwards, Brian H., *Revival! A people saturated with God*, (Welwyn Garden City: Evangelical Press, first published in 1990 and now available through Day One Publications).

5   Ibid., p. 26.

6   Another book that includes a more personal account of such a time is, *Under the Thorn Tree*, (Fearn, Ross-shire: Christian Focus, 2017), by the late Richard Bewes.

7   The comments come at the end of the interview when she is told that she will have the Bible on 'her desert island'. *Desert Island Discs* – Aung San Suu Kyi - BBC Sounds

8   For example, in Genesis 3:15, 21.

9   From the hymn, 'More about Jesus would I know', by Eliza Edmunds Hewitt (1851–1920). https://www.hymnal.net/en/hymn/h/382

Chapter 9

1   https://assets.publishing.service.gov.uk/government/uploads/system/uploads/attachment_data/file/897289/countryside-code-leaflet.pdf

2   While this does not appear to be in the actual Hippocratic Oath, it is tied so closely to it that, in 2015, a joint report by the British General Medical Council and Medical Schools Council was entitled, 'First do no harm: enhancing patient safety teaching ...' https://www.gmc-uk.org/education/standards-guidance-and-curricula/position-statements/first-do-no-harm---enhancing-patient-safety-teaching-in-undergraduate-medical-education

3   I don't have access to the original place that this was written or even a book by Isobel Kuhn, a missionary to China (1901–1957), in

which it was quoted and have relied on: https://barbaraleeharper.com/2007/03/27/a-sense-of-him/

4 Mangalwadi, Ruth and Vishal, *Carey, Christ and Cultural Transformation*, (Noida, India: OM Publishing, 1993), from Chapter 1.

5 Mangalwadi, Ruth and Vishal, *Carey, Christ and Cultural Transformation*, p. 5.

6 Ibid., p. 8.

7 Bewes, Richard, *Under the Thorn Tree*, p. 110.

8 Ibid., p. 105; https://en.wikipedia.org/wiki/Anthony_Ashley-Cooper,_7th_Earl_of_Shaftesbury

9 https://www.christianitytoday.com/history/people/missionaries/william-carey.html

10 Edwards, Brian H., *Revival! A people saturated with God*, p. 26.

11 https://www.oxfordreference.com/view/10.1093/acref/9780191826719.001.0001/q-oro-ed4-00010671

12 With thanks to Above Bar Church, Southampton for the idea of this cycle.

13 From memory someone from the Pocket Testament League

Chapter 10

1 https://en.wikipedia.org/wiki/What_Katy_Did.

2 Edwards, Brian H., *Revival! A people saturated with God*, p. 238.

3 I remember the line from seeing him on television many years ago: https://www.jimmycricket.co.uk

4 Edwards, Brian H., *Praying for Revival*, available from Day One Publications, 2019.